Lessons from the Hearthstone Traveler

An Instructional Guide to the Creative Thinking Processes

by Bob Stanish

illustrated by M. Nature

Cover by Tom Sjoerdsma
Copyright © Good Apple, Inc., 1988
ISBN No. 0-86653-433-4
Printing No. 987654321

GOOD APPLE, INC.
BOX 299
CARTHAGE, IL 62321-0299

**This book is dedicated
to the memory of**

**Bob Eberle,
friend, mentor and colleague.**

Credits

Foreword:
Gary A. Davis

Photographs:
Frank Crocker
Jon Stanish
Bob Stanish

Art:
Mother Nature

Computer Art:
Bob Stanish

Reviewers:
Marsha Mason
Cindy Haskett
Carol Singletary

Foreword

It is a pleasure to introduce a book about creativity written by someone with the exciting imagination of Bob Stanish. *The Hearthstone Traveler* is a marvelous addition to his series of fine guidebooks for stimulating creative thinking in the classroom.

The ideas in this unique volume extend far beyond just strengthening through exercise such traditional creative abilities as fluency, flexibility, originality and elaboration. Stanish presents creativity-related principles and exercises designed, for example, to help the student develop self-understanding, take other points of view, see patterns and relationships in nature, relax and concentrate, write sensitive cinquains and other poetry, visualize and transform, invent humorous gadgets, evaluate ideas with meaningful criteria, use the highly effective Osborn/Parnes creative problem-solving model, and much, much more . . . .

The author well understands that metaphor plays a key part in creative thinking. *The Hearthstone Traveler* introduces the synectics methods, using these and other metaphor-based exercises to strengthen the student's ability to make connections and see relationships, that is, to think metaphorically. The book also includes a collection of other idea-finding techniques including brainstorming and brainwriting and several variations of these. Attribute listing, idea checklists and forced combinations, all strategies used by creative people, also are included. Humor, a common trait of people who play with funny ideas and possibilities, is properly encouraged.

Stanish has a unique talent, stemming no doubt from his own creativeness, for illustrating how new perceptions and idea combinations may be generated almost effortlessly. Throughout, the material is lively and captivating and prods one, for example, to make sounds like a period, comma, question mark or parentheses, or to create an invention to do housework or deliver pizzas. *"Take from within this book what travels well with you,"* says Stanish in the epilogue. Any creativity-minded teacher will be able to take much, for *The Hearthstone Traveler* is rich in content and ideas.

Gary A. Davis
University of Wisconsin

Table of Contents

Foreword iii

Introduction vi

Photographs and Statements x-1, 18-19, 28-29, 50-51,
68-69, 82-83, 96-97,
116-117, 125-126

Activity Sections
    Cinquain and Infinity 2
    Seeing 6
    In Touch with the Reflective Self 12
    In Touch with the Emerging Self 14
    Meanders, Branching, Explosions and Spirals 20
    Mindstretching 30
    Viewing Self and Others Through Symbolic Analogies 34
    Metaphorical Thinking and the Inner Window 38
    Springboarding Ideas 44
    Discovering by Doing 52
    Springboarding Individual Ideation 56
    Structure, Randomness and Haiku 70
    The Unnumbered Page . . . .
    Random-fit and Problem Solving 74
    Analogy Card Game 77
    Diamante and Duel Ideating 79
    The Next Unnumbered Page . . . .
    Igniting Originality Through Humor 84
    Guiding Fantasy Towards Expressive Poetic Language 98
    Symbolizing Self 104
    Brainstorming: Some Varied Ways 108
References 118
Index 123

Introduction

The Hearthstone Traveler is a guide to the creative processes of this day and time.

To you who are classroom teachers, a special note . . .

It was but a few years ago that I decided to re-enter a public school classroom again. Not having been a classroom teacher for well over a decade, it became a special experience of meaning, insight and reflecting, continuing thought.

The strategies in this book reflect changes in education, the developing child and attitudes toward teaching as I perceived and reacted to them—sometimes in frustration and sometimes in joy.

I have come from this experience with, indeed, great respect and appreciation for the classroom teacher. I have come from this experience with great empathy and admiration for the creative teacher—and it is to both, with love, that this *Hearthstone* is given.

It is becoming more difficult to stimulate student productive thinking through oral questioning.

Causing students to generate ideas in a classroom, I believe, is more difficult today than it was a decade ago. Having been nurtured by the visual benefits of a technical society, students are not just receiving information by an auditory process alone. In fact, the auditory may not be the primary means of processing information for most children. With many children the visual image is the prime stimulator for creative imaginative thought.

*Visualizing, imaging and the integration of modification techniques within ideational strategies are used in this book for stimulating productive student thinking.

Student opportunities to engage in divergent thought are minimal in many schools.

Within the present structure of education there are pressures to increase test scores. The way it is being done is through memory and convergent processing. Being able to think productively requires a whole mind approach. A whole mind is a blend of critical and creative thinking.

*The diverging-converging pattern of productive thinking has been deliberately planned in this book.

A child is a being of feeling and thought. But family time to the child is being diminished by strong economic and social factors.

Today, teaching encompasses more than teaching. Counseling, perhaps mentoring, and adjunct parenting are not duties assigned but duties assumed.

Who, in teaching, has not seen tears of sorrow?
Who, in teaching, has not heard words of despair?
Who, in teaching, has not been touched by the complexities within
    a living child?

Having a home may satisfy a need for secure shelter, but it does not necessarily satisfy the need to feel secure. Self-esteem building and identity-building require some sense of belonging—some sense of importance.

***An effort is made, in this book, for students to formulate metaphorical
        associations—
        of self to others,
        of self to this planet,
        of self to the universe,
        of self to the universe
            within.**

It is for the child that we attempt to provide.

Due to the wide polarity of student differences within classrooms, there is no single educational package, method, model or curriculum that can accommodate all realistic and desirable educational objectives.

Large publishing firms compete in competitive markets for their textbook adoptions. Yet, teachers in their personal search for educational materials basically created another market—that of small but emerging publishing firms. It is interesting to note that this market was created by one of the lowest salaried levels of certified professionals in society. This, in itself, announces a need to accommodate the complexities with a classroom—complexities born from the changing structures of a society.

*There are variations and approaches in this book that can accommodate some instructional needs with some children. The most appropriate usage is that of selection for a given reason— a given time.

And finally . . .

*There are some statements derived from notes kept of my sojourn back into a classroom. They began as open letters from one member of a faculty to a faculty. They require, I think, no clarification. They are of this day and time . . .

Looking
at early morning sunlight
on my patio is an experience.

Through silhouetted shapes and existing forms,
I see sunrays dance.

It is breathtaking to my mind and time.

Ideas are like this.
They can dance in our minds like flickering
rays of sunlight.
Some are extended and widened; some lose their identity
but reappear in a different shape;

a different form.

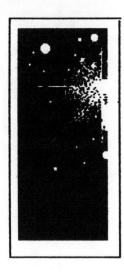

Cinquain and Infinity

Galaxy

Star island

Glowing, swirling, stretching

Inspiring, yearning, sombering, brooding

Nebulae

It is more than possible to gain glimpses into our own creative infinities.

Capture the essence of a cinquain in this way:

1. Brainstorm words associated with your selected title.

2. Brainstorm a second list of words that are descriptive of the title. Make these words *ing* words.

3. Brainstorm a third list of feeling words. Make these words *ing* words, as well.

- Write the title on line one.

- Select two words associated with the title and from the first brainstormed list for line two.

- Select three *ing* words that are descriptive of the title from the second brainstormed list for line three.

- Select four *ing* feeling words from the third brainstormed list for line four.

- Go back to the first brainstormed list and select a word associated with the title for line five.

Consider the variations on the next page.

Options:

1. Consider these titles for either individual,
   team or total class effort:

   twilight
   morning
   serenity
   dream
   frost
   snowflake
   star
   earth
   moon
   shoreline
   seashell

2. As opposed to brainstorming lists, consider the concept of **brainwriting**.
   Place students in small groups with one piece of paper per group. Silently
   they write words associated with the directions on the previous page.

3. Consider the application of drawn charcoal images in association with
   individual cinquains.

4. Use the concept of cinquain to capture the essence of a reading
   assignment.

5. Use the concept of cinquain to capture the biographical essence of a
   personality studied.

6. Research the origins of cinquain.

7. Discuss why the brainstorming of *feeling* words seemed more difficult
   than brainstorming the other two lists of words?

8. Try two-person readings on two different cinquains at the same time.
   In other words, one person reads one line of his poem. The other person
   then reads one line of his poem. Continue alternating until both poems
   are read.

9. Write cinquains about self. Use one's first name on line one and the last name on line five.

10. Write cinquains as a conclusion to a unit of study or a chapter of a text.

Brainwriting originated from the Battelle Institute in Frankfurt, Germany (VanGundy, 1981). Brainwriting functions with the same basic rules as brainstorming except the responses are written.

RULES:

- Silently and individually write an idea to a problem on a piece of paper.

- Pass the written idea to the person sitting on the right.

- Use the idea received in one of three ways:

> Use it to stimulate another idea, write it on the paper and pass it to the right.

> Modify the idea received; write it on the paper and pass it to the right.

> Write a completely different idea on the paper and pass it to the right.

Ideas keep circulating on paper in a rotating fashion for several minutes. Upon completion, pin them to a bulletin board or tape to a wall for easy access.

Within the present structure of public education, I know of no greater reservoir of resourcefulness than that displayed by the highly creative teacher.

An Important Note:

Beginning on page 108 is a collection of **brainstorming techniques**. Although this list is not complete, it is believed by this writer that by varying ways to promote student ideation in classrooms, a broader range of intellectual talent is accommodated.

When the word *brainstorming* is seen throughout the activities in this book, peruse the approaches available. It is also recommended that several of the techniques be combined within a single idea-generating session, if time and energy are available.

The works of Arthur B. VanGundy (1981, 1984) is of special mention. VanGundy, a human relations specialist on the faculty of the University of Oklahoma, has compiled a variety of ideation techniques and brainstorming methods utilized by business and industry. There appears, in my opinion, opportunities to use many of these techniques in classrooms and school organizational offices everywhere.

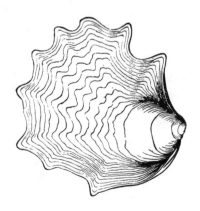

Seeing

An Exercise:

At a moment in time, take your students into a nearby field or woods with pencil and paper.

Tell them to let their eyes fall on whatever is in front of them. It may be a leaf, a sprig of grass, a twig or even a portion of a plant—just something small and manageable.

Tell them to close their eyes for several seconds and lose whatever lingering thoughts are within their minds.

Have them open their eyes and focus again on what they observed.

Tell them to **look at it with such concentration that it appears to look back.**

Encourage them to **imagine the item** they are seeing **is the most important thing on this planet**—a rarity within the universe.

Have them take their pencils and draw the item—draw it without looking at their papers. **Let the pencil caress and hold in the mind what is really seen.**

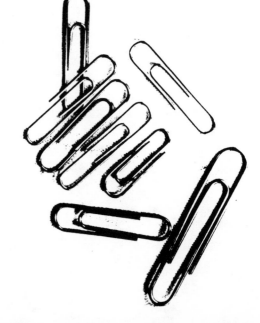

To really see is a kind of visual caressing with unwavering attention. This can lead to contemplation and to the fullness of acceptance and of knowing.

Encourage them **not to let their eyes wander** from the item being drawn. Tell them to allow the lines and texture of the item to enter their minds and to capture the essence of its being. **Draw the lines very slowly and lovingly.**

Just follow what the eyes see.

Afterwards, place the drawings on a classroom wall.

Allow each student to **share his experiences and the attributes of the item drawn.**

Options:

1. Write a cinquain next to the drawn item.

2. In what ways might the **attributes** of the drawn item be used to improve something totally different?

3. Discuss the meaning of this: *To really see is to accept.*

4. Look at some photographic copies of paintings by Van Gogh or Rembrandt. Try to imagine their process of "seeing." In what ways, do you suppose, it was unique?

5. Can a distinction be made between *see* and *seeing?*

Attribute Listing was developed by Robert Crawford (1954) in the 1930's. According to Crawford's premise, new ideas originate from previous ideas modified in some fashion (refer to item 2). A ratchet screwdriver, as an example, was created by altering one of the attributes of the common screwdriver—the turning of the handle being replaced by the pushing movement of the ratchet. According to J. P. Guilford (1977), attribute listing enhances writing, invention, planning and problem solving.

Imaging the Here and Now

Imaging is nurtured, I think, by relaxation and stimulation. I enjoy taking the basic forms of nature and allowing my mind and pencil to caress the image into extensions well beyond the subject. Sometimes the extensions may suggest solutions to a variety of problems or maybe the design is just simply pleasing to my mind and time.

Take a pencil or a pen and very slowly extend the lines into a different realm. Do not attempt to determine beforehand the image. Just allow the lines you add to extend from the provided lines. Afterwards, attempt to analyze the image you created. In what ways does it describe you? In what ways might it be established as a goal or stated as a problem to be solved?

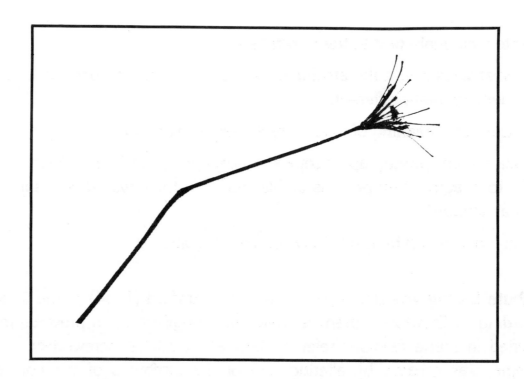

Once taking two grasses laden with seed, I made a machine copy of them. Extending the lines, a wooded scene appeared. In searching for a meaning, I reflected on the day and the days before. I recalled the demands and the pressures and the decisions made. I walked on a woodland path that day.

Here are some more images to extend. Find a day when quietness and introspection are in order.

Just remember to allow yourself time. Allow your eye and hand to caress the beginning image. Rid your mind of existing concerns and delay judgement only until the box is complete.

The act of creativeness requires both creative and critical thinking skills. It is a blend—an incredible blend of beauty.

Joe Khatena has done extensive work with imagery. Of particular interest is *Imagery and Creative Imagination* (Khatena, 1984). Khatena's book contains a number of exercises for developing imagery skills, several of which are usable with the creative problem-solving and synectics processes. Also highly recommended are Robert H. McKim's book, *Thinking Visually: A Strategy Manual for Problem Solving* (McKim, 1980) and Frederick Franck's, *The Zen of Seeing: Seeing/Drawing as Meditation* (Franck, 1973).

Options:

1. Several of the photographed life-forms in this book are simple office machine copies of collected items. Some are examples of a destruction-reconstruction process, that is, taking apart one life-form and adding the parts to another for a different synthesis. Often the new synthesis offers associations and new perspectives to the mind. And quite frequently the stimulation to write and compose poetic verse occurs.

   Try the process!

2. Put together images of natural forms for stimulating haiku, tanka and cinquain.

3. Try machine copy collages of natural life-forms. Alter aspects, if necessary, through the concept of destruction-reconstruction. Add aspects such as color, ink or whatever comes to mind.

   Try making a machine copy collage of self. Use analogy statements associated with the materials used. Examples:
   I am a grass stem because . . .
   I am like a seed because . . .
   I am like a shell because . . .

   Advice: Turn the light control setting to a very light reading.

4. Using words of imagery to stimulate visual imagery:

First, select a phrase that encompasses a present mood:

shadows on a reflecting pond
dancing rhythms of sunlight
life-forms of awakening wonderment
windswept plains
endless journeys

Second, look at this item from different angles. Allow the mind to stimulate images from the provided image. Select the image that connects with the phrase and complete the drawing by extending lines and images. Then ask yourself, are there changes I need to consider? Alterations I need to make? Questions I need to explore? Maintenance I need to ensure?

In Touch with the Reflective Self

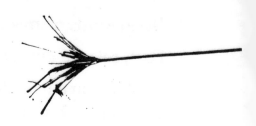

1. Suppose your home was afire and there was only time to retrieve one nonliving possession.

   I would retrieve_____ because

   _____

   _____

2. A verb that would presently describe me would be _____

   I selected this verb because _____

   _____

   _____

3. The most important thing I would share with anyone would be _____

   _____

   I would share this because _____

   _____

   _____

4. I daydream most about _____

   _____

   _____

5. Something that most people know about me is _____

_____

_____

_____

Something that few people know about me is _____

_____

_____

6. I am most happy when _____

_____

_____

7. I am most unhappy when _____

_____

_____

8. The most difficult statement to complete on this exercise was _____

_____

It was difficult because _____

_____

_____

_____

_____

_____

In Touch with the Emerging Self

1. When I double my present age, my most important nonliving personal possessions will probably be

   _____

   _____

   _____

   _____

   _____

2. List as many nouns as you would like to become.

   _____   _____

   _____   _____

   _____   _____

3. The most important achievement I would hope to achieve is _____

   _____

   It would be important because _____

   _____

   _____

   _____

4. Eventually, I will probably have
   . . . an unlisted telephone number
   . . . an answering service
   . . . a listed telephone number

   because _____

   _____

   _____

5. The three most important things in my future will probably be _____

   _____

   _____

   _____

6. As an adult, I probably will be known for (circle one):

   being social   being independent
   being imaginative   being trustful
   being in control   being a sound follower
   being a risk-taker   being happy-go-lucky
   being conscientious   being shrewd
   being competitive   being practical
   being able to get along with others   being confident
   being sensitive   being hard to fool
   being a leader   being realistic

   I believe this will be true because _____

   _____

   _____

   _____

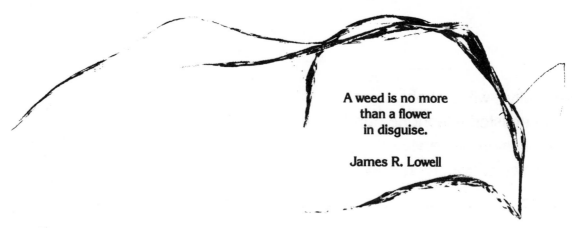

A weed is no more
than a flower
in disguise.

James R. Lowell

"In Touch with the Reflective Self" and "In Touch with the Emerging Self" are indicators of self-image, of self-esteem, of the extending and emerging self, of values and of the general realm of the affective domain. The blend of thought, feeling, learning, and application are crucial to the expansion of human creative potential. Providing open-ended statements in which responses are not judged but clarified are extremely helpful to students.

Appropriate clarifying responses should also be nonjudgmental. Some examples of the clarifying response would include:

What makes this important?
Can you expand on this thought?
Where do you suppose this will lead?
What will be the effect of this?
Can you give some examples?
Can you explain this in more detail?
What other choices did you consider?
What do you anticipate will occur?
What will be the consequences?
Is there another way of explaining this?
How might this affect others?
How did you arrive at this?
Am I hearing you say (paraphrase the statement)?
What are some of the advantages? Disadvantages?
What makes this valuable?
What other approaches are available?

Why questions have a tendency to cause a respondent to become defensive. Questions that extend the premise and explore available choices are more valuable to the respondent.

Options:

1. Consider taking individual questions from each activity and administering them singularly on a periodic basis. Consider readministering the same questions at a later period in time for a comparative analysis.

2. Consider utilizing the response sheets for individual conferences with students.

3. Compare your opinions of each child with the opinions stated by each child. Are there ambiguities and paradoxes?

4. Consider doing a public interview with a child in a classroom, using the format of these open-ended statements. Establish rules beforehand like:

   - No talking by observers
   - The right to pass on any statement or question
   - The right of the respondent to end the interview

   The interview would be extremely beneficial in helping students affirm beliefs and opinions on value-related topics.

5. Take a question like number 6 from "In Touch with the Emerging Self" and have each student respond to the item silently. Then have each student attempt to guess, in writing, how other classmates responded. Share the results with each student.

> "How do I know the way of all things at the beginning?
> But what is within me?"
>
> Lao Tzu

Walk So Gently with Me in These Woods Nearby

Child, take my hand and walk so gently with me in these woods nearby. We shall see the patterns of the universe and the universe within. We will reflect what is and what was and that of tomorrow, too.

Look closely at this lichen on this fallen branch. It is a tiny pattern of explosion like the wood violet and the sudden light of a firefly and a mind cell within you. And in the night sky of space, within each island galaxy, the pattern is repeated.

Look closely at this dry ground and see the branching lines of erosion. Allow your eyes to caress and follow the lines. And above you, see the tree. For it branches, too. And within you are neurons—a branching system of tributary axons and dendrites. You are a river, and within each galaxy there are rivers of space. And within these woods is a river that meanders. And see the dry sand whose granules follow the explosion form of the wood violet. Here is a sand print of a moving snake. For it too meanders in its movement of life.

And touch this mushroom and feel with hand and eye the texture and curvature of its beauty. It is the curvature of space and time. For it is the spiral and it is of this galaxy in pattern. And it, too, repeats itself within you and these woods.

Stay here, for awhile, and caress what is and what was and that of tomorrow, too.

Meanders, Branching, Explosions and Spirals

There is an exercise of several days. I hope it promotes for you the essence of the universe as it did for me.

Before beginning, a few definitions are in order.

A meander is a pattern that doubles back on itself. It extends itself with twists and turns. Rivers are meanders and so are the ridges of the human brain and so is a plant vine that clings to a tree.

Branching is an extension or network pattern that becomes increasingly smaller as it extends from its nucleus or core or basic body. A tree's branches and the branching of tributaries from a river and the network of arteries and veins within us are of this pattern.

An explosion is a pattern whose paths extend from the center to every extended point. A sunflower, a starfish, the brilliance of a supernova and the splatter of paint on a surface are explosion patterns.

A spiral is a pattern that wraps around itself. In doing so it creates a special withinness that is different from its surroundings. Certain seashells and spiral galaxies and hurricanes are of this shape. Many of the spirals of this universe come in opposite pairs and many are turbulent.

Listed on the next page are numerous events which lead to a greater understanding of ourselves and our tiny planet within the island galaxy of the Milky Way. Do not attempt all the events, but do several of your choosing. Before embarking, read to yourself, "Walk So Gently with Me in These Woods Nearby."

meanders

branching

explosions

spirals

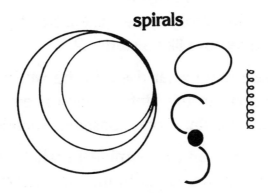

Directions: Present definitions and the sample patterns of a meander, branching, an explosion and a spiral to your class. They are to embark upon an investigation—an investigation as to the repetition of these patterns throughout our world and the microscopic world, within the structures of their human structures and throughout the universe as we understand the universe.

Select from these events:

- Collect from plant forms examples of the four patterns. Do this at home or school or in a field or in a woods. Bring the sample plant forms into class and place them on a clear plastic wrapping. Place the wrapping on the school's photocopy machine for a picture. The clear plastic wrapping will keep the pieces intact and eliminate cleanup concerns. Select reference books on the human anatomy, that is, respiratory system, circulatory system, skeletal system, nervous system and digestive system. Select pictures from these resources that would reflect the four patterns. For example, the circulatory system would provide the heart and the arteries and veins (branching) of the system. Select reference books that would display our knowledge of the universe and select those pictures that would reflect the four patterns. For example, the Milky Way Galaxy is a spiral. Do the same with reference books on life within the seas. For example, a starfish is a good example of an explosion pattern. Make photocopy pictures from the references selected. Students should then group the pictures into groupings that reflect the four patterns. Place the groupings on poster board. After doing so, then ask:

  . . . In what ways is a clam like a galaxy?
  . . . In what ways is our circulatory system like a tree?
  . . . In what ways is a supernova like a starfish?

- Look at maps and determine what rivers in the world seem to meander the most? In this country? In this state? Which rivers are meanders and branchers? In what ways do states and coastlines meander?

- Look at topography maps and determine in what ways do mountains branch. Which mountains appear to branch the most? In what ways do they assist rivers in their branching?

- Look through microscopes at protists. In what ways do they resemble the four patterns?

- Look at the skeletal systems of animals. Look at the root systems of plants. Compare the branching of skeletal systems with the branching of root systems. List as many similarities as you can.

- Problem-solve ways to capture the structure of a spider's web. Look at the way it extends and defines itself as a branching system.

- From the business and financial pages of discarded newspapers, create a collage of line graph meanderings. How do they fit the description of a meander? At what points were the financial graph meanderings beneficial or less beneficial to investors?

- Look at lunar landscapes and landscapes of Mars and Jupiter and Saturn. What patterns do you see?

- Create aerobic dances to music that would define the pattern of a meander, branching, an explosion and a spiral.

- Consider haiku and tanka as examples of meandering thought. Look for examples and write originals that reflect the meandering stream of consciousness. Consider poetry that has surprising, startling or unusual twists as conceptual examples of explosions. Find some examples. Write some examples. Consider cinquain as an example of branching—the extension of graphic form into a branching pattern. Write some examples. Consider some of the statements associated with the photographs in this book as an example of branching. Write some examples.

- Look at star maps in reference books. Find constellations whose space between planetary bodies would reflect meanders. Look at ocean currents from the pages of atlases and other references. Find the currents that reflect the closest definition of a meander.

- Refer back to "Imaging the Here and Now" in this book. Use the design listed under Options and extend the branching and meander patterns into patterns of explosions and spirals. What do the completed pictures appear like? Where would you expect to find a similar pattern? On distant planets? Within a human cell? Speculate.

- Refer back to the definition of a spiral, that is, the special withinness in particular. Ascertain the special withinness of these special forms:
  a tornado
  a clam shell
  a galaxy
  the human ear
  star sapphires—a spherical algae
  delicate ascidians
  the vortex of a tropical storm
  snails
  blue water plankton
  human blood cells

Extend the identification of spiral forms and determine the special withinness of each.

- Investigate the human windpipe as a branching pattern. Determine how it branches into the lungs and how each hollow branch divides into smaller and smaller branches. Then refer again to the definition of branching.

- Investigate the pattern of branching in the rib cage and the pattern of branching from the heart and how it branches again and again into smaller and smaller extensions.

- Investigate the patterns in architectural structures such as:
  the branching framework of load-bearing walls
  steeples that spiral
  multi-family housing units that meander
  dome stadiums that spiral
  bridges and branching

- Investigate the use of spirals in machinery designs
  . . . in computer art
  . . . in Van Gogh's paintings
  . . . in fashion designs
  . . . in the human face
  . . . in the horns of animals
  . . . in floral patterns
  . . . in whirlpool patterns
  . . . in religious temples

- Investigate how many garden flowers have spiral blooms
  - . . . at home
  - . . . at a florist shop
  - . . . in a park
  - . . . growing wild in a woods

- Using paper, iron shavings and magnets, create a magnetic field into one of the patterns. Which pattern was easier to create? Why?

- Using tree limbs and twine, create a branching structure on the school grounds to accommodate eight people.

- Taking regional or city road maps, determine the branching and meadering lines.

- Many spiral forms come in opposite pairs. Investigate and report on left-handed and right-handed bacteria, on left-handed and right-handed DNA and on binary stars. Place a hand mirror on a photograph of yourself so that the left side of the photographed face has a full image. In other words, the left side is imaged as a whole face. The mirror should be placed in the center of the photographed face and adjusted at an angle. Repeat the process with the right side. What are the contrasts? What interpretations can be made from this demonstration and the concept of opposite pairs?

- Using materials that are capable of becoming meanders, create weavings. Consider materials such as twine, grasses, and ropes.

- Experiment with dough and bake bread that displays the twists and turns and other attributes of a meander or bread that displays the attributes of a spiral. How many cookie recipes call for designs that are explosions? Create a new explosion pattern with homemade cookies.

- Brainstorm solutions to a given problem. Phrase the question like, "In what ways might we . . . ? Record solutions on the chalkboard or on paper, then web the solutions provided into common categories of thought. Afterwards, ask: "In what ways is creative thinking like a branching system?"

- Study the clockwise movements of storms above the equator and the counterclockwise movements of storms below the equator. How would these occurrences associate with the "opposite pair" concept of certain spirals?

- Study the hemispheric differences, left and right, of the human brain. What kinds of comparisons can be drawn with clockwise and counter-clockwise movements of storms above and below the equator with the hemispheric functions of the human brain?

- Using silver and gold sequins, glue and black poster board or black construction paper, create spiral galaxies. Place the silver sequins by the nucleus of a galaxy. Refer to reference books on astronomy or space for photographs, paintings for ideas. Investigate information on galaxies to accompany each mosaic pattern.

- Using a definition of a structure such as . . . **a structure is something that takes up space and accommodates material,** then the four patterns are structures. See how many structures can be named in which one or more patterns are a part of that structure. For example: a river with meandering and branching; a flowering plant with explosion and branching, etc. Expand this notion of a structure. Is a sentence a structure? Is an atomic particle a structure? Is a family a structure?

- Use the patterns to extend affective awareness like:
  I seem to meander when . . .
  I am like an explosion when . . .
  I seem to branch when . . .
  I am the paired opposite of some spirals when . . .
  My thought meanders whenever I . . .
  My mind is like an explosion when . . .
  My thought branches when I think about . . .
  Like a spiral, I have a special withinness on the subject of . . .
  One of my favorite keepsakes is a (name the pattern) because . . .

Options:

By adding to some of the suggested events, an interesting instructional unit could materialize. If the inclination is to do this, consider these **generalizations and objectives.**

Generalizations: 1. There are basic patterns found on this planet, in the universe and within ourselves. Some of these repetitive patterns are meanders, branching, explosions and spirals.

2. Patterns either by themselves or in unity with other patterns and forces form structures.

3. A structure is something that fills space and accommodates material.

Objectives: (The first numeral refers to the generalization.)

1.1 Students will identify the patterns of a meander, branching, explosion and a spiral from:

    1.11 available references on the human structure of systems, organs and cells

    1.12 available photographs of the universe

    1.13 available references on nature and natural forces

    1.14 available references on structures created by man

1.2 Students will classify forms and forces into the following categories:

    meanders
    branching
    explosions
    spirals

1.3 Students will cite and create associations and analogies between studied patterns. The associations and analogies shall include:

    selected and discovered life-forms
    selected and discovered man-constructed forms
    selected and discovered universal forms and forces

1.4 Students will make application of learned understandings by (list the verb and the activity), for example, creating collages, constructing models, collecting data, writing poetry, . . .

2.1 Students will identify combinations of patterns, each dependent on the other, within a given entity. These combinations or unities will be discovered from:

    2.11 available references on the human structure of systems, organs and cells

    2.12 available references on the universe

    2.13 available references on nature and natural forces

    2.14 available references on the construction of structures by man.

2.2 and 3.1   Students will define a structure as something that fills space and accommodates material.

2.3 and 3.2   Students will classify structures according to their pattern or combination of patterns. Combinations formed shall be formed from the cited patterns.

We Are, at Times, Like Prairie Grass upon a Landed Sea

Into the central plains, as far as the eye could see, stood prairie grass of great stature. The grass caressed the ground and made rich the soil. And with the wind it shimmered and waved much like a sea.

Settlers came and claimed the land and upon it established herds of grazing animals. The land also was tilled and upon it were placed plant forms of various kinds. Prairie grass grows no more on the land it once caressed.

Including and beyond the central plains, as far as the eye can see, are the dwindling lands of the caring fields. Our days are spent here and our nights are in preparation of the days. And to those who neglect the child and to those whose ambitions exclude the child, we say to them, "We are at times like prairie grass upon a landed sea."

Mindstretching

Analogies may open windows of new understandings, glimpses of differing relationships and the extensions of our creative beings.

1. Which has more stretch—forgetfulness or helplessness?

_____ has more stretch because

_____

_____

_____

_____

2. Which is louder—sunrise or sunset?

_____ is louder because

_____

_____

_____

_____

The important thing on these analogies is not the answer given but the explanation.

30

3. Which is quieter—failure or embarrassment?

_____ is quieter because

_____

_____

_____

_____

4. Which has more bounce—a book or a tennis ball?

_____ has more bounce because

_____

_____

_____

_____

5. Which is more lasting—lost or found?

_____ is more lasting because

_____

_____

_____

_____

Synectics is a technique created by William J.J. Gordon. Innovative solutions to problems are sought through reversing things—making the strange familiar and the familiar strange.

There are four kinds of analogies associated with the synectics process (*Making It Strange*, 1968, Books 1-4).

- **personal analogy**: Requires identifying oneself with a process or object. The losing of one's identity allows for imaginatively looking at things from differing points of view. "If I were a bottle cork how would I react to the expansion of internal pressure?"

- **direct analogy**: Requires a comparison between associated facts in different disciplines. "Could we learn to build better shopping malls by studying anthills?"

- **symbolic analogy:** Requires an image aesthetically satisfying as a means of looking at a problem—a bonding of metaphors. "Imagine a telephone that is like a pleasant secretary dealing with unpleasant business."

- **fantasy analogy:** Requires making connections with the world as we know it and where anything is possible. "If we could use trained dolphins to monitor home swimming pools, what kinds of pool specifications would we need?"

6. Which is more restful—a circle or a straight line?

_____ is more restful because

_____

_____

_____

_____

The analogies in this section are basically direct analogies. The answers are not important but the explanations are. Look for unique kinds of associations. As an example, some possible responses for item 6 might include:

A circle is more restful because there is no beginning or an end—no need to rush. A circle may represent an orbital path in which other forces are at work.

A line is more restful because in a horizontal position it is lying down. The quickest route between two points is a straight line. A straight line will arrive in less time than a curve or a square and therefore would have time to rest.

Options:

1. Try a direct analogy for conceptual understandings within a given subject area. For example, which has greater vision—fiction or nonfiction?

2. Try analogies as a closure on a lesson. For example: "In what ways is a beehive like a closed society? In what ways is a butterfly like a mixed fraction?"

3. Look for visual analogies as they may be inferred from paintings, especially those of Picasso, Klee and Wood.

4. Listen for analogies in the musical works of Copeland, Strauss and Springsteen.

5. Draw an analogous symbol of self.

6. Discover the beauty of written analogies in haiku and cinquain.

7. Use analogies to explain the positive attributes of others. For example: Paul's mind soars like an eagle. Janet's imagination is more vivid than starlight.

Viewing Self and Others Through Symbolic Analogies

They are referred to as symbolic analogies by synectics. Prior to that they were called oxymorons. In either case, they are combinations of two incongruous terms like *sharply foolish* or *mournful optimist*. What is interesting about them are meanings and understandings inferred. When directed towards the affective self they may provide new perspectives of certain events and behaviors in our lives in which commonly used words fail.

Directions: Respond only to those items that appear important to you.

1. I experience **deafening silence** whenever _____

   _____

   _____

   _____

   _____

   ____ frequently   ____ not so frequently   ____ somewhere in between

2. I experience **joyful sadness** whenever _____

   _____

   _____

   _____

   _____

   ____ frequently   ____ not so frequently   ____ somewhere in between

3. I experience **busily lazy** whenever _____

_____

_____

_____

_____

___ frequently   ___ not so frequently   ___ somewhere in between

4. I experience **shyfully popular** whenever _____

_____

_____

_____

_____

___ frequently   ___ not so frequently   ___ somewhere in between

5. I experience **controlled excitement** whenever _____

_____

_____

_____

_____

___ frequently   ___ not so frequently   ___ somewhere in between

6. I experience **attentively ignored** whenever_____

_____

_____

_____

_____

___ frequently   ___not so frequently   ___somewhere in between

7. I experience **openly closed** whenever _____

_____

_____

_____

_____

___ frequently   ___not so frequently   ___somewhere in between

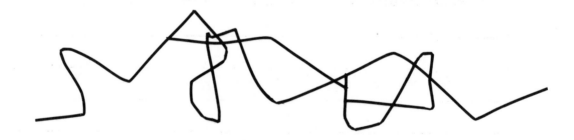

Questions to think about:

1. **Do I have a need to gather more information?**

2. **Do I have a need to share some thoughts and feelings?**

3. **Is there a problem here? If so, how might I state the problem?**

4. **Do I need some help, if there is a problem?**

Options:

1. It would appear that the preceding format would assist students in identifying problems of a social nature. The very nature of symbolic analogies or oxymorons reflects internal conflict with the combined opposite meaning words. The major emphasis intended here is to provide a teacher with an alert system.

   Guidelines:

   - **Encourage students to infer their own meaning with each paired symbolic analogy.**

   - **Encourage students to see you for a private conference, if needed.**

   - **In conference with a student, use clarifying responses to assist students in identifying more specifically the problem and alternative solutions.**

   - **If professional help appears needed, contact parents, and if available, counseling services.**

2. Symbolic analogies are extremely useful in setting the general perimeters of **story writing.** Since they embody internal or compressed conflict, they make ideal working titles for stories. Consider, as a beginning step for written narratives, your class generating or brainstorming a listing of direct analogies, for example: lost victor, cooperatively competitive, unscholastically scholastic, etc. By doing this, the conflict that requires resolution in a story is there with the working title. Change the working title, if desired, at some later time.

Metaphorical Thinking
and the Inner Window

The creative strength of metaphorical thinking may be used in innovating existing products, the creation of new products, generating classroom skills in the use of the analogy, creating insight for thinking and writing and looking at self in introspective kinds of ways.

These particular questions are for the purpose of discovering new understandings of self. Who am I? Where am I now? Where have I been? Where might I go from here?

1. In what ways has my life been like a river?

_____

_____

In what ways has my life been like a mountain?

_____

_____

In what ways has my life been like a tree in a forest of trees?

_____

_____

I would rather be a _____ because _____

_____

_____

2. Think in terms of how these items function and the purposes they serve.

   a candle
   a rubber band
   a doorknob

   Which of the three would best describe you? _____

   In what ways are you like this item? _____

   _____

   _____

   If you could improve the item, what improvements would you make?

   _____

   _____

   Think about how the same improvements might apply to you.

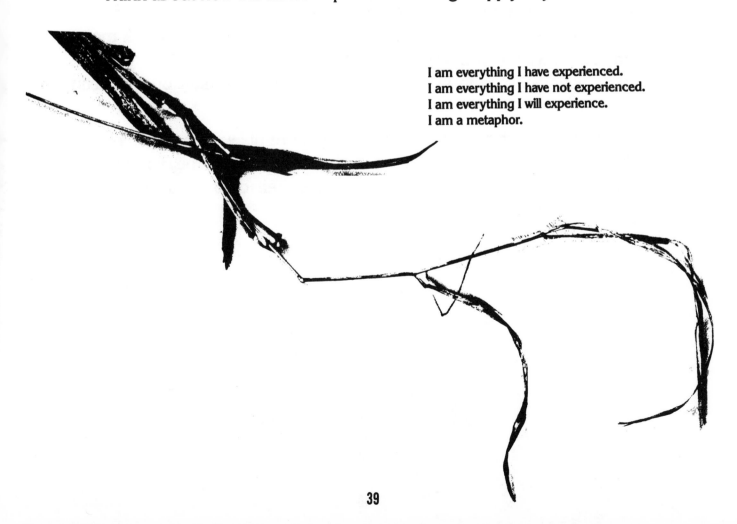

I am everything I have experienced.
I am everything I have not experienced.
I am everything I will experience.
I am a metaphor.

3. Metaphorical Thinking and Problem Solving

Suppose a personal problem might be: In what ways might I assert myself at work so that my opinions are heard?

Begin by personifying objects and life-forms into problem statements in this way:

If I were a sponge, in what ways might I assert an opinion?
If I were a tuning fork, in what ways might I assert an opinion?
If I were a hawk, in what ways might I assert an opinion?
If I were a song, in what ways might I assert an opinion?
If I were a magazine cover, in what ways might I assert an opinion?

Some possible responses might be:

Absorb the opinions of others and respond in an associative fashion.
Vibrate or repeat your opinions when possible.
Circle or move around when addressing others with your opinions.
Wait until the group mood is silent or melancholy or happy **like a mood created by a song or melody**, then state opinions.
State your opinions in writing in an **eye-catching fashion** on a bulletin board or wall.

Expanding possibilities is done by adding more "If I were . . ." statements. Try to express the idea with a word or phrase symbolic of the metaphorical statement. Select those possibilities that reflect the attributes and possibilities within the inner self.

4. Study the choices below and then select the one that most accurately describes you.

*Use E as a combination of textures or for the establishment of a different texture.

The texture of my present feelings is _____
because

The texture of my present thoughts is _____
because

The colors of my feeling texture are _____

The colors of my thought texture are _____

The touch of my feeling texture can be described as

_____

The touch of my thought texture can be described as

_____

Maslow suggested that self-actualization and creativity are but the same. Others have too.

Knowing the texture of teaching today, it is as important to nurture the creativeness of those who teach as it is those who are taught. The actualization of self makes for better teaching and for better learning.

For an effective understanding of metaphorical thinking, refer to the works of Gordon (1961), Gordon and Poze (1972) and Prince (1982). For an effective summation of metaphorical thinking and its application in classrooms, see Davis' *Creativity Is Forever,* 2nd edition (1986).

Metaphorical thinking, as I define it, **is the ability to take a concept into different or new contextual settings for the purpose of gaining unique understandings.** The context may not only offer new glimpses of the idea or problem or to the solution of that problem, but glimpses into our selves— our inner windows.

Options:

1. Review item 4 and try the concept of shapes and personal goal setting. My goal setting is most like a square, a squiggle, a circle, a straight line, etc.

2. Again, based on the concept of item 4, try:

   What might my bed say to me, if it could give me a message?
   What might my watch say . . . ?
   What might my favorite possession say . . . ?
   What might my favorite chair say . . . ?
   What might my shoes say . . . ?
   What might my ears and eyes say . . . ?
   What might my stomach say . . . ?

   Are any of the messages similar?

3. Express your thoughts and feelings in writing by assuming the role of one of the following from the listing below. Afterwards, think or tell about a possible life experience in which similar thoughts and feelings could occur.

a piece of transplanted driftwood whose function now is a conversation piece on a table

a windblown seed that matures into a plant where others of its kind do not grow

a willow tree root searching for the riverbank of a drought-affected stream

a diamond being cut and polished into a glistening stone

an eagle feather being carried by air currents as it descends to earth

clay being molded into pottery

a new banjo string joining others of its kind

a mirror that faces a front door

a frozen strawberry being defrosted in a plastic container

a volunteer corn plant growing in a field of wheat

a sugar maple leaf losing greenness and gaining the color of yellow-orange

a flat key on a piano in the process of being tuned

Springboarding Ideas

By modifying the angles of viewing and sensing, ideas may multiply by incredible numbers.

As an example, take a common form like a simple paper clip and a desire to improve and innovate both the appearance and the function. First of all, for purposes of creative thought, let's focus on the image of a pipe cleaner. A pipe cleaner can be made into a paper clip rather easily.

Take some pipe cleaners with the intention of improving the function of a paper clip and allow some of these questions to stimulate your inventiveness.

1. In what ways might you bend the shape into a different design? Reshape? Triangular? Rectangular? Circular? Something else?

2. In what ways might you combine two into a different design? Three? More? Combine with something else?

3. In what ways might color be used? One color? Combine colors?

4. In what ways might something else be added? A pattern? Odor? A magnetic substance? Initials?

5. In what ways might it serve additional purposes than originally intended? Personalize? Symbolic design? Contain a message? Additional functions and reasons for being?

6. In what way might it be reduced? Cut in half? Something less in length?

7. In what ways might it become larger? Firmer? Stronger?

8. In what ways might the texture be improved? Softer? Coarser?

"Springboarding Ideas" is the utilization of the **idea checklist**. There are several outstanding ones. Alex Osborn's **seventy-three idea-spurring questions** (1963) and Eberle's *Scamper* (1971), a variation of the Osborn model, and the Davis and Houtman (1968) variation of the Osborn model are especially recommended.

Sometimes the idea checklist is referred to as **modification techniques or strategies**. The basic premise here is that of modification for improvement or innovation. In an educational setting it is frequently used for viewing things in different ways for additional understandings.

Bob Eberle built a mnemonic device into the word *scamper* in order to apply many of Alex Osborn's idea-spurring questions in practical and easily remembered ways. Scamper was originally embodied in a series of imagination games written for young children, but the uses are incredible in providing the s-t-r-e-t-c-h for new ideas in all realms and ages. Consider some of the suggestions in the Options section for extending the uses of an idea checklist.

Schools should accommodate creative inventiveness. It may take invention of the highest order to find solutions to the problems we and our forebearers have created on this planet. Basic skills are indeed necessary, but it is the accommodation of the creative mind that serves mankind in all the realms of knowing and doing.

*SCAMPER CHECKLIST

Substitute
To have a person or thing act or serve in place
of another. Who else? What else? Other place? Time?

Combine
To bring together, to unite. Combine what? Bring who
together? Combine purposes? Ideas? Materials?

Adapt
To adjust for the purposes of suiting a condition.
Reshape? Tune up? Tone down? Accommodate? Agree?

Modify—Magnify—Minify
To alter, change form or quality. Other color? Sound?
Motion? Form? Size? Shape? Taste? Odor?

To enlarge, make greater in form or quality. Add what
to make higher? Stronger? Thicker? Longer?

To make less, to minimize. Make what smaller?
Lighter? Slower? Less frequent? Shrink? Reduce?

Put to Other Uses
Use for purposes other than originally intended.
New uses as is? Other places to use? Use when? How?

Eliminate
To remove, omit, or get rid of a quality.
What to cut out? Remove? Simplify? Weed out?

Reverse and Rearrange
To place opposite or contrary. Turn what around?
Upside down? Inside out? 180° flip?

Change order or sequence. Other pattern? Layout?
Plan? Scheme? Regroup? Redistribute?

*Bob Eberle, *Scamper-On for Creative Imagination Development* (1984).
Printed with permission of D.O.K. Publishers, Inc., East Aurora, N.Y.

Options:

1. Try lyric composing with young children using scamper. As an example, substitute a key word from a familiar song; then write lyrics that would accommodate the substituted word. From "Row, Row, Row Your Boat" substitute a word like *walk*. And from the checklist, *What else?* How about a dog? So, "Walk, walk, walk your dog gently down the street." Complete the entire song in this fashion. The value of this is that children can see other avenues for generating ideas, avenues for extending ideation into realms of fun and enjoyment. Fun and enjoyment has transfer to the real world of problems and conflicts if the processing is skill related. See an article entitled "Songwriting Should Be Taught in Your Gifted Program" (Skaught, 1987).

2. Consider using an idea checklist for the purposes of analyzing deliberately distorted events and situations. Minify: Suppose Lincoln's stature was that of Douglas (Lincoln-Douglas debates). In what ways could this have impacted on the course of American history? Rearrange: Suppose Michaelangelo painted the walls of the Sistine Chapel as opposed to the ceiling. Speculate on the ramifications of this. Put to other uses: Come up with one hundred different uses for a coat hanger. Magnify: Suppose the population of rabbits increased by one hundredfold. How might this affect life on this planet?

3. By applying idea checklists towards innovating and improving things, inventive ideas are nurtured. Switch parts? Combine functions? Change shapes? Different size? Make stronger? Remove something? Exaggerate something? Make it faster? Use a different material? Change color? Increase stability? Improve performance? Lower costs?

4. Richard de Mille (1955) and Eberle (1971) used the concept of idea checklisting to write imagination games for children. A de Mille and Eberle type of imagination game would be similar to the version on the next page. The . . . indicates an intended pause during the reading.

A Light Beam

Imagine a desk lamp. Switch on its light. Stretch its neck and beam out a light. Beam it on the wall . . . Beam it on the door . . . Beam another one on the floor. Make them swirl . . . Make them dance . . . Sit on a light beam . . . Was it somewhat extreme? . . . Slide down a light beam . . . Was it like a jet stream?

Imagine an elephant that's very big . . . One that even wears a wig. Make an elephant shadow with your beam. Cause your beam to make it jig . . . Imagine a giraffe that's very tall . . . One that's photographic . . . Make a giraffe shadow with the same old beam. Isn't this a wonderful scheme? Combine the two shadows into one . . . Isn't this fun? What do they look like? . . . That is, two into one from the beam that was done. Did they look ghostlike or to your dislike? . . . Make the shadows swirl and make them dance . . . This is an opportunity to take a chance. What do you think of giraffaphant shadows? Did they give you a different slant for making shadows?

Find a lion that's fairly bold. Create another shadow from a safe stronghold. Make the shadow swirl and make it dance . . . Cause some flail with its skinny tail . . . Grab the shadowed-tail and swing like a monkey in every detail . . . Swing higher and higher but don't you fail. Just fall on a rainbow that's right over there. Just slide down the rainbow like you did on the beam . . . That is the theme. When you use your imagination you're sure to grow. You certainly won't fit the status quo!

the end

The above imagination game was designed through the *Scamper* checklist using basically the processes *of substitute, combine, adapt, modify* and *put to other uses.* Application of this concept may be accomplished in several ways using the processes involved. For example, draw strange zoo creatures by *combining* the attributes of two or more animals. Create shadows through the light beam of an overhead projector with combined items or objects. Cause the items selected to project a shadow suggesting something else (*put to other uses*). Have students pretend they are walking through various suggested substances *(modify)* such as a room full of peanut butter, a room full of Jell-O, a room full of honey, etc.

A parody is writing in which the language and style of an author or work is closely imitated and exaggerated for comic effect. Use the idea checklist to help structure parodies on how Dr. Seuss might respond to a few contemporary issues, for example, "The Untradeable Tradeables (trade imbalance), The Pockethole Porkbarrel Torks (national deficit)," etc.

5. Idea checklists, as much as anything, help with the application of principles and processes. Be it the modification of spoons or modification of squares (Torrance, 1979) or even paper clips, checklists are of great value. I personally have found them invaluable to stimulating the creative processes with children and adults in classrooms and training sessions.

Checklists are, of course, associated with **brainstorming**. It may be of value here to review briefly the origins of **classical brainstorming**.

Brainstorming as a group method for problem solving was developed by Alex Osborn in the late 1930's. Osborn wrote extensively on the importance of imagination and creativity in solving problems. In his classic, *Applied Imagination* (1963), he cited several concepts to enhance the development of creative thought. Among the most valuable is that of **deferred judgment**. Deferred judgment is the separation of two processes—the process of generating ideas from the process of assessing ideas. In other words, first generate a multitude of ideas because among them will likely be truly useful, innovative and workable ideas. This concept is referred to as "quantity breeds quality." Judgments made during the "free-flow" of ideas will only derail the motivation for making them. Two other significant concepts inherent within the Osborn model is that of making associations and using creative techniques deliberately.

Osborn had **four basic rules for brainstorming:**

- **Criticism is ruled out.**
- **Freewheeling is welcomed.**
- **Quantity is wanted.**
- **Combining and improving are sought.**

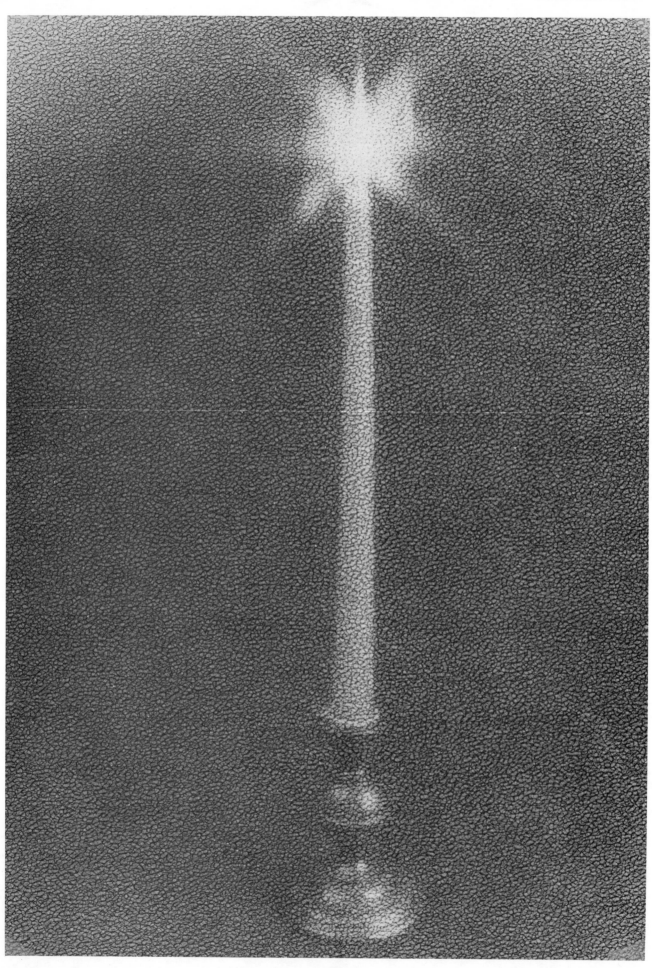

I remember not the teacher who assigned the exercise.
I do remember the teacher who cherished and cared for
me when I worked the exercise.

I am a by-product of her starlight—her nova.
I am the by-product of all those who have shared their
novas with me. I carry their starlight.

And through my burst of starlight is their starlight.
It is within my being. I am because of them.

Discovering by Doing
Adventures in Scavenging and Problem Solving

1. Create a device that will produce a giant soap bubble.

   Experiment with detergents and mixtures. Investigate the attributes of soap molecules and discover a way to measure the diameter of a giant soap bubble.

   I discovered that _____

   _____

   _____

   _____

   _____

   _____

   _____

2. Determine a way to capture and bring to school the structure of a spider's web.

   I discovered that _____

   _____

   _____

   _____

   _____

   _____

   _____

3. Collect and identify flower petals and the leaves of herbs. Dry them in garages or brown sacks or microwave ovens. Place the dried leaves in jars and create a potpourri.

I discovered that _____

_____

_____

_____

_____

_____

4. Create a weaving from natural grasses and fibers.

I discovered that _____

_____

_____

_____

_____

_____

5. Create a poster of natural-colored stains from living plants.

I discovered that _____

_____

_____

_____

_____

_____

6. Create original cookies by combining pieces of favorite candy bars with favorite breakfast cereals into a standard mixture for baking.

I discovered that _____

_____

_____

_____

_____

_____

7. Using soaked dried peas as connectors and toothpicks or straightened-out paper clips, create a model of a geodesic dome.

I discovered that _____

_____

_____

_____

_____

8. Do a crayon rubbing on the inscription of the oldest and the most interesting epitaph you can find.

I discovered that _____

_____

_____

_____

_____

Advice on

Discovering by Doing

Do not assign the entire exercise at one time. Consider, as a weekend homework event, one activity or a student choice of one per page. Spread the entire exercise out over a span of months. Encourage the written reactions to the *I discovered* statements.

On soap or surfactant molecules: These molecules have heads that are attracted to water and tails which are repelled by water. One of the attributes of surfactant molecules is that they quickly join together to close openings. By taking a thin metal rod and soaking it thoroughly in the detergent mixture, one can penetrate a large soap bubble without bursting it. Thus, the diameter of the bubble can be measured in this way.

On capturing the essence of a spider's web: There are several ways of doing this. The easiest way is to use clear plastic Con-Tact paper.

The important thing on any of these exercises is to encourage students to make their own discoveries.

Options:

1. Consider, as a regular part of the school year, providing activity type scavenger hunts that promote investigation and discovery.

2. Encourage the concept of discovery journals that begin with "I discovered...."

> "But there are those (and they are few)
> who see much more than others do."[1]

[1]Nathan and Janet Levy, *There Are Those* (1982). Printed with permission of N.L. Associates, Inc., Hightstown, New Jersey.

Springboarding Individual Ideation

This concept was used in *Mindglow* (Stanish, 1986). During my most recent experiences with children, it became apparent that the ideational fluency techniques I used in the past required some modification. The modifications incorporated extended the visual and sensory realms of selected topics for additional ideation.

Directions to students:

The starfish design, like many other designs, can cause our minds to become inventive. Listen to these statements and write down ideas as they appear in your mind. I will read the statements slowly and, if time is available, make a sketch of some of your more interesting ideas.

What you are being asked to do is to list as many new and different invention ideas as you can for a starfish design.

1. What could you create with this design if you tied the arms together? What could it be? Turn the design over. What could it be?

2. What could you create with the design if you filled it with air? If you filled it with water? If you filled it with something else? What could it be?

3. What could you create with the design if it could be worn? What could it be?

4. What could you create with the design if it had a fragrance or odor? What could it be?

5. What could you create with the design if it could be carried? If it could carry something? What could it be?

6. What could you create with the design if it could be hung on a wall? If it held something while attached to a wall? If it had pockets while attached to a wall? What could it be?

7. What could you create with the design if it could be squeezed? If it contained something while being squeezed? What could it be?

8. What could you create with the design if it became smaller? If it became tiny? What could it be?

9. What could you create with the design if it had wheels? What could it be?

10. What could you create with the design as an ornamental? What could it be?

11. What could you create with the design if it could be taken into the woods? The mountains? A stadium? On a picnic?

12. What could you create with the design if it was larger than a house? What could it be?

13. What could you create with the design if it was placed on a ceiling? In a living room? In a bedroom? On a lawn? What could it be?

14. What could you create with the design if it was in an aircraft? On a body of water? In space? In an automobile? What could it be?

15. What could you create with the design if it was multi-colored? Changed color? Had no color? What could it be?

16. What could you create with the design if it was smooth? If it was spongy? If it was coarse? If it was leakproof? If it had holes? If it was sticky? If it was hot? If it was cold? What could it be?

Intermission: Take a break at this point and let students consolidate and share their thoughts. Encourage the concept of piggybacking. **Piggybacking** is the combining of two or more ideas into a different or improved idea.

We must teach the skills of thinking. To say time is not available is to say the information that is being taught is all inclusive and not subject to change.

17. What could you create with the design if it could float? If it was spongy? If it could bounce? If it could sail? What could it be?

18. What could you create with the design if it could be thrown? If it had wings? What could it be?

19. What could you create with the design if one arm was removed? More than one? What could it be?

20. What could you create with the design if it had a zipper? If it had buttons? What could it be?

21. What could you create with the design if it was confined to a desktop? Inside a drawer? What could it be?

22. What could you create with the design if it was attached to twine, rope or chains? What could it be?

23. What could you create with the design if it could accommodate a battery? A light? A sound? What could it be?

24. What could you create with the design if it was to be placed in a box? What could it be?

25. What could you create with the design if one or more arms was extremely long? What could it be?

26. What could you create with the design if it could be played? What could it be?

27. What could you create with the design if it had handles? Straps? A hook? What could it be?

28. What could you create with the design if it was clear plastic? Styrofoam? Ceramic? Rubber? What could it be?

29. What could you create with the design if it was small enough to be placed in a purse? A billfold? A pocket? What could it be?

30. What could you create with the design if there were hinges on the arms and it could be folded and stored? What could it be?

31. What could you create with the design if there were legs under the arms? What could it be?

32. What could you create with the design if it turned on an axis? Rotated in both forward and reverse positions? Were taken apart and reassembled? What could it be?

Again, allow time for the consolidation and sharing of ideas. Encourage the piggybacking on the ideas of others for a different or improved idea.

Introduce or provide the idea evaluation grid on page 62 to students. An **idea evaluation grid** is a means by which ideas may be rated in association with a selected criteria.

The problem is: In what ways might I use a starfish design to create a unique and original product.

Have students arbitrarily select their ten best ideas and list them on the grid, A through J.

The idea evaluation grid can accommodate up to five criteria. The criterion items are to be written at the top of the grid in a staircase pattern. With older children and adults, encourage criteria to be brainstormed; then select the ones deemed most appropriate. For younger students provide assistance. Some criterion items that would fit most situations are provided here and on the next page.

Criterion Items

acceptance by others?
adaptable to situation?
advantageous?
agreement of those concerned?
appealing; attractive?
assistance available?
attitudes (positive) about idea?
behavior (positive) towards idea?
beneficial?
commitment: long-term?
commitment: short-term?
consistent?
cooperation available?
cost-effective?
cost-efficient?
cost for start-up reasonable?
challenging; holds interest?
creative solution?
creative enhancement?
(not) dangerous?
deadline can be met?
(not) distracting?

ease in doing?
effect: immediate?
effect: long-term?
effect: short-term?
efficient?
economical?
endorsement from key people?
explainable to others?
financing available?
fits situation?
flexible to situation?
functional?
imaginative?
improve a condition?
improvement: long-term?
improvement: now?
improvement: short-term?
interest will expand?
lasting effect?
manageable?
markets available?
materials available?

materials and cost?
measurable results?
needs met?
organizational acceptance?
operational?
performs well?
performance over time?
policies fit?
practical?
predictable?
prevents _____?
price?
produces desired result?
profitable?
reasonable or logical?
resources available?
results immediately given?
results: long-term?

results: short-term?
rewarding to others?
rewarding to self?
rewards?
risks: low?
safety?
situation appropriate?
socially acceptable?
success likely?
time?
time: efficient use of?
timely?
transfer?
transferrable to other situations?
useful?
values in tact?
valuable?
works consistently?

For purposes of the activity the following criteria might appear usable: Adaptable to situation? Affordable? Appealing or attractive? Beneficial? Cost-effective? Not dangerous? Ease in doing? Explainable? Fits situation? Imaginative? Materials available?

Criterion items on this page and the preceding page can fit a wide variety of problems. Use them accordingly.

Have students determine or select five criteria to evaluate their ten best ideas. Each idea is given a point value as measured by each of the five criteria. The ideas with the highest point totals would therefore be the most promising.

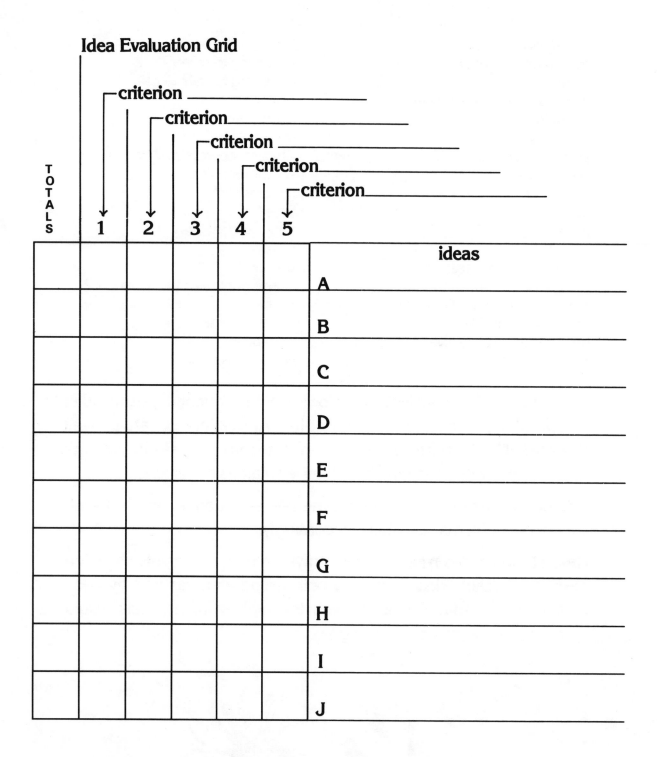

Idea Evaluation Grid

criterion _____

criterion _____

criterion _____

criterion _____

criterion _____

TOTALS

	1	2	3	4	5	ideas
						A
						B
						C
						D
						E
						F
						G
						H
						I
						J

3 points = excellent
2 points = good
1 point = average
0 point = below average

Creative
Problem Solving
Step by Step

Using the steps of creative problem solving on the problem cited on page 56 (*In what ways might I use a starfish design to create a unique and original product?*) would be like this:

Mess Finding	Accepting the challenge of creating an original starfish design; determining that it can be done; visual imaging of the design
Data Finding	Gaining information on what needs to be done; investigating the shape and attributes of a starfish; investigating various types and kinds
Problem Finding	This is the statement of the problem. *In what ways might I use a starfish design to create a unique and original product?*
Idea Finding	This step involves generating or brainstorming many solution ideas. The use of brainstorming in many of its varied forms is encouraged.
Solution Finding	Making use of an idea evaluation grid with selected criteria, see pages 60 through 62. The most promising ideas are selected for creating a starfish design and a decision is made.
Acceptance Finding	A plan to implement the solution is prepared.

For an overview of the **Osborn-Parnes Method of Creative Problem Solving (CPS)**, see *Creative Problem Solving: The Basic Course* (Isaksen and Treffinger, 1985). In teaching the skills of creative problem solving in classrooms, see *CPS for Kids* and *Be a Problem Solver* (Eberle and Stanish, 1980 and 1984). For extensive training in creative problem solving, write to **The Creative Education Foundation**, Inc., 437 Franklin Street, Buffalo, New York 14202 and inquire about the annual **Creative Problem-Solving Institute (CPSI).**

Options:

1. As an appropriate application for problem solving, have students follow through with the process and create an innovative product using their best idea as selected from criteria.

2. The larger pictures of the starfish are ventral views and the smaller pictures represent a dorsal view. By either side a starfish is a marine echinoderm of the class Asteroidea, that is, characteristically having a radially symmetrical form with five arms extending from a central disk.

   By what associations can you associate a starfish:

   > ... with a professional baseball team?
   > ... with entities in space?
   > ... with a flower?

3. In what other forms and titles may the design of a star be found? Speculate on why some designs are found in nature over and over again in different species. Speculate on the transfer of this design into our lives and the lives of those who preceded us, for example, emblems, symbols, etc. Speculate on this: Whatever design man created was here prior to man.

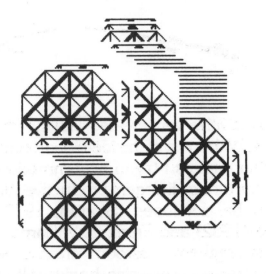

There are many and varied ways of looking at things.

4. Investigate the habits, habitat and characteristics of starfish.

5. If a starfish specimen is available, notice how the fissures line up three by three in the center of the body and perpendicular at the perimeter edges. Compare this arrangement with that of a pinecone. Speculate on what brings patterns of this kind into being? Is it the close packing of cells? Is cracking involved? Is it wrinkling? No one, as of this writing, knows for sure.

6. Extend the fissure pattern of a starfish into other distinct patterns found in nature. Refer to "Meanders, Branching, Explosions and Spirals" in this book. Investigate the use of hexagons in nature or the three corners of a triangle that can be made into a hexagon. Fuller exploited this concept with geodesic domes. In what other ways are patterns from nature used by man?

7. How many different geometric shapes can be produced by combining triangles? Build three-corner triangles with toothpicks and soaked dried peas as connectors. After the designs have been created, investigate their names.

A Summary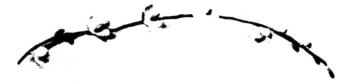

As can be surmised, the previous two activities were created with the structure and the expansion of an idea checklist. With most of the ideational techniques I design and use are several important factors I try to accommodate. I do this because it is my belief that by nurturing divergent-productive thinking, specific creative thinking skills can be developed (Stanish, 1977). The pioneering work of E. Paul Torrance (1962) and Frank E. Williams (1970) inspired the efforts I've made to strengthen classroom creative abilities through teacher idea books. Many classroom exercise books still provide for these **factors of creative thinking:**

- **fluent thinking:**   The ability to think of a *large quantity* of ideas.

- **flexible thinking:**   The ability to think of *different* possibilities or approaches.

- **elaboration:**   The ability to *embellish*, provide *detail* and to *expand* on a given subject.

- **originality:**   The ability to offer *unique* and *different* approaches.

It should be noted that elaboration is the most difficult of the factors to judge. There is a tendency, at times, for individuals to overembellish. Creativity, I think, is also knowing when to stop and this may be of an intuitive realm. I doubt if Hemingway would have achieved the fame he did if he over-embellished the succinctness of his style. Henry Moore's sculptures as do the paintings of Georgia O'Keefe reflect this essence of not overembellishing a product. This skill, and it is a skill, is reflected in the products of so many highly creative people.

It also appears that another skill of prime importance to divergent productiveness is that of **visualization,** that is the ability to process images in the mind. The potential here is that images may lead to ideational transfer and application. The works of de Mille (1967), Eberle (1971, 1982, 1984), Khatena (1984) and McKim (1972) are of special mention. The questions associated with "Springboarding Individual Ideation" are structured to promote mental images leading to ideational fluency.

J.P. Guilford's (1967) research (**Structure of the Intellect Model or S.O.I**) into the nature of the human intellect provided insights into creative behavior and its expression. Divergent thinking is the generation of multiple ideas including the unusual and the unique from a given stimuli. **Divergent production** requires multiple responses as opposed to **convergent production,** where the attempt is to find a single best response. Creative thinkers generally excel in the divergent process.

A category of divergent-production abilities is that of **transformations** in the S.O.I. model. This processing is basically that of making alternative changes. These abilities, it would appear, would contribute to creative thinking due to the flexibility and fluency factors of thought. Transformations are further subdivided into visual transformations, symbolic transformations, semantic transformations and behavioral transformations.

Children who are high creatives, it would appear, would benefit from teachers who are also high creatives. However, creativity can be accommodated in any classroom regardless of the creative intelligence of the teacher. It is a matter of providing, in addition to other provisions, exercises that accommodate the factors of creative thinking and exercises that extend imagery and imagination.

There is no single mold for teaching.

There is no single mold for anything.

A school may try to create one
and a state may try to mandate one
but the essence of teaching lies within
your essential self.

Imagine the essence of Christ
and the use of the parable.

Imagine the essence of Socrates
and the use of the question.

Imagine the essence of Buddha
and the use of meditation.

Teach with the essence within your essential self
and the method is there.

Structure, Randomness and Haiku

Haiku has three unrhymed lines of a syllabic pattern. The first and third lines have five syllables each. Seven syllables are contained in the second line.

> Provide randomness during the processing of creativity and it will be integrated into the order.[1]

Try this approach to writing haiku. **First**, think of a topic. A topic might consist of a plant, an insect, a season, a natural element, an event, a memory, a thought, etc. **Second**, brainstorm attributes associated with the topic. **Third**, allow a remote and random event to enter your consciousness. **Fourth**, brainstorm thoughts and feelings associated with the remote and random event.

Example:

Topic: a willow tree

Attributes associated with the topic: spreading, yellow spikes, willow limbs, branches, shading, swaying, weeping, water-seeking roots, etc.

Event entering consciousness: a merry-go-round

Thoughts and feelings associated with remote and random event: childhood, swirling, spinning, summer ride, idle time, moving, up and down, etc.

[1]Bob Stanish, "The Underlying Structures and Thoughts About Randomness and Creativity," *The Journal of Creative Behavior,* 1986, 20 (2), 110-114.

Write the 5-7-5 syllabic poem from the words brainstormed. Use them freely. Add additional words if desired.

Willow limbs spreading.
Swirling, moving, summer ride.
Idle childhood dreams.

Suggestions from promoting random events:

- Allow movement to enter your consciousness. Allow the movement to formalize into something visualized in the mind.

- Open a dictionary, and without looking, point to a word. Select a definition and allow that definition to suggest something tangible. If the word is an article, a preposition, or something not useable, repeat the procedure again. Use the random word to generate associated words.

- Leaf through a book on art. Take notes on some of the suggestions stimulated in the mind. Select one of the suggestions. Use the suggestion to stimulate words.

- Listen to music. Allow the music to promote a symbolic image. Use the symbolic image to generate words.

- Recall a recent dream. Use the recall to generate an event in that dream. Use the event to stimulate words.

- Go for a walk, stop at something small and interesting, for example, a spider's web. List *ing* words associated with the item.

> **Random-fit:** The accommodation and integration of random concepts within a structure.

The above term is of my invention. It applies to my perception of the usefulness, continuance, flexibility, and development of a structure. It would appear that the continuance of any structure is dependent upon its ability to accommodate randomness. Structure is meant to infer both physical and metaphysical entities. Hence, relationships, organizational patterns, syntax, distinct problem solving and other processes would be interpreted as structures.

Options:

1. Consider using the concept of *random-fit* with tanka. Tanka has a syllabic pattern of 5-7-5-7-7. It is the addition of two lines of seven syllables each to the haiku structure.

2. Try the concept of random-fit to the improvement of things. In other words, what randomly selected words could offer meanings that might improve a grocery shopping cart? A refrigerator? A chair?

3. Try specific content topics and random-fit for haikus and tankas to analyze student synthesis and understanding of subject matter. Topic examples: parallelograms, narrative, collective bargaining, closed circuit, open society, etc.

4. Use haiku, without random-fit, to capture the essence of a famous painting or sculpture. Use haiku to capture the essence of commercial advertising. Use haiku as an observing technique. For example, include the attributes of seashells in a haiku.

> There appears to be a unified order to everything. It encompasses both structure and randomness. Structures change because of their abilities or inabilities to accommodate randomness. When structures decay they become random and subject to inclusion or rejection by other structures. (Stanish, 1986, JCB)

The Unnumbered Page

Use this unnumbered page for transfer or extension.
In terms of what I've read, what might fit into the way I
teach? In what I teach? Into who I am or want to become?

Continue on to the next unnumbered page.

Random-Fit and Problem Solving

Causing the "aha" experience can be deliberate. Ideas can be stimulated from a variety of sources, especially from words.

Take a word like *expressway*. Expressway has several definitions, but suppose we allow the word to function in our minds as a highway. The function of an expressway in this context is that of travel—travel that may be uninhibited by stops and delays. It carries the potential of arriving at a destination in less time than from taking different routes.

Suppose I have a problem associated with congestion in a school library—too many students and not enough resources. Stated as a problem, we have: **"In what ways might we utilize our library to accommodate the number of students we have?"** Facts associated with this problem might include limited resources and scheduling problems and limited space.

Going back to the random word, *expressway,* some possible solutions may be formulated. How about "road sign" posters placed high on shelves indicating the type of resources in that location. Would this cause less congestion among students? How about the association of expressway rest stops and areas designated for study, for example, areas placed away from the "expressway" of bookshelves?

But don't stop with *expressway.* Select another word in a random fashion for a random-fit. A word like *exit* might enter one's consciousness from an exit sign above a door. Try the same procedure and add those ideas to the ideas generated from the first word.

What happens when a word doesn't seem to fit? Disregard the word and try another. Develop a criterion and select the solutions that appear practical and possible.

Options:

1. Try random word meanings to improve existing household appliances. Select words on the basis of a sequence, for example, every tenth word on the far right-hand column of a dictionary page with a letter from your name. If the word is an article, prefix, suffix, conjunction, etc., try a different word. Use one of the meanings associated with the word to suggest improvement of the item.

   Suggested items for improvement:

   > a refrigerator
   > a microwave oven
   > an iron
   > an electric can opener
   > a dishwasher
   > a washing machine
   > a dryer
   > a blender

   Create both explanations and drawings of the improvements made.

2. With administrative approval, determine an acknowledged problem existing within your school. In addition to brainstorming possible solutions, use random words to suggest additional solutions. Begin the problem statement with "In what ways might we . . . ?" Select the best answers using the idea evaluation grid and suggested criteria from pages 60 to 62.

3. Use content word meanings to suggest improvement of existing items and things. "In what ways might the atomic structure of carbon suggest improvement in establishing learning centers?" Select content words in a random fashion from a textbook index.

4. Excursions to stimulate writing among problem writers.

Allow for daydreaming on guided fantasies, but do not provide too much guidance. Example: Take a trip from the east coast to the west coast. Allow for images of scenic events to build in your mind. After two or three minutes, stop the excursion and have students respond in writing with some of their recall.

Provide some phrases such as like a forgotten promise, like yesterday's dream, like an image remembered, like a resurfaced feeling, like a lingering concern, like the calmness after a storm, like the passing of sorrow, like an awakening truth. Create more if you like. Let students bond a written image from their excursion to one of the provided phrases.

Having a sentence completed, ask these questions:

What kinds of events might lead to a feeling statement like you have written?

What kinds of events might follow a feeling statement like you have written?

See if you can write a page around the sentence.

See if you can write a story around the page.

Note: The randomness of excursion events applied to provided words may facilitate more interesting departures from the ordinary. Use techniques of this kind occasionally. One of the more difficult aspects of writing is *how to begin.* There are no set ways to writing. The beginning of a story may very well be the conclusion. We inherently think there are sequential steps to everything. Ask some practicing scientists about the scientific method.

Analogy Card Game

Preparation: Paste pictures taken from magazines and newspaper ads onto index cards. Pictures should include general purchasable items like automobile tires, furniture, computers, tools, clothes, etc. Prepare one picture per card.

Select a student referee whose function is to judge responses and keep time.

The game is to be played by four to six students. Twenty-four cards per game are adequate.

Directions: The person with the nearest birthday in the group shuffles the cards and places them face down. The person on the shuffler's right goes first and draws two cards and places them face up. This person lists as many analogies or comparisons as he or she can between the two items within a sixty-second time limit.* The referee may judge a response invalid.

*Make adjustments on time limit due to age and maturity of players.

Play continues until all students have drawn twice. The student with the most unchallenged responses wins.

Response Example: Suppose two cards drawn have pictures of an automobile tire and a houseplant. Two possible analogies might be: *Rubber comes from a plant and a tire is made from rubber or tire treads and leaf veins both consist of lines.*

Options:

1. Consider making photocopies of key personalities or pictured concepts from a textbook and paste them to index cards for insertion in the Analogy Card Game deck. *In what ways is Benjamin Franklin like an automobile tire?* Possible answers: Franklin's thoughts and good automobile tires have a tendency to wear well. Franklin's face is on currency and it takes currency to purchase tires. *In what ways is the U.S. Constitution like a shirt?* They both can be mended (amendment). They were both manufactured by persons, etc.

2. Use analogy formats for review of chapters, units and important elements within a curriculum. *In what ways is a sentence like a river?* They both have a tendency to run, to flow, to alter direction, etc. *In what ways is an improper fraction like a school desk?* Analogies extend thought in so many wonderful directions.

3. Encourage students to help you create additional cards by bringing to school pictures of both interesting and common items.

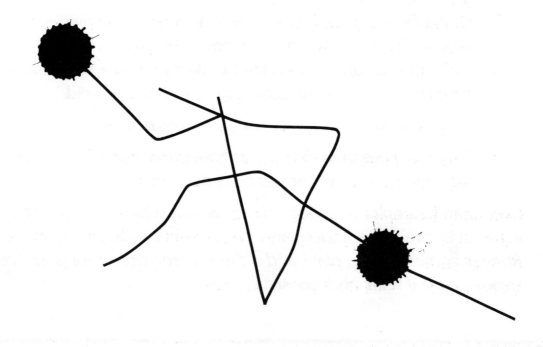

Diamante and Duel Ideating

Diamante is a reverse poem of seven lines. It provides an interesting interplay of words and sequence.

line one . . . .   one noun
line two . . .   two adjectives
line three . . .   three participles
line four . . .   four nouns
line five . . .   three participles
line six . . .   two adjectives
line seven . . . one noun

Study this example.

Loud
noisy, screaming
blaring, screeching, piercing
ambulance, police, people, street
stopping, crowding, staring
stunned, mournful
silence

Notice the diamond figural design of the poem.

Notice how the nouns of opposite meaning, *loud* and *silence*, converge into a holistic pattern within the poem's context.

Directions:

1. Provide two noun antonym topics to two paired students.

2. One student is to brainstorm separately as many words as he can associate with one of the paired nouns. The other student is to do the same with the opposite word.

3. Taking the words generated separately, have the two students work together in combining some of those words into a diamante. **Remind** them to

use the structure of the diamante. **Remind** them to converge with words the opposite-meaning nouns into a blending process, where the fourth line is neutral to the lines above and the lines below.

4. As a beginning point, provide paired nouns like *north* and *south, bad* and *good, sharp* and *dull, reality* and *dream, acceleration* and *deceleration, divergence* and *convergence, beautiful* and *ugly, tall* and *short, black* and *white, health* and *sickness, hot* and *cold, sun* and *moon, won* and *lost,* etc.

Options:

1. Consider using the diamante in composing poems about well-known adversaries. Consider names and titles like Hamilton and Burr; Democrat and Republican; any two, past or present, presidential candidates; two opposing athletic teams; two competitive commercial products; etc.

2. Consider using diamante on strong value issues like church and state, censorship and free speech, Creationism and Darwinism, armament and disarmament, nuclear and nonnuclear, etc.

The Next Unnumbered Page

Use this unnumbered page to create a statement about yourself in a graphic way. Think in terms of a flower that's unique and one of a kind or think in terms of a rainbow with colors aligned in a different way or just simply play with an image of tomorrow rather than today.

When you are with children
for a long, long time,
it is like hearing the seeds and buds growing

or

seeing the creation of a snowflake design before
it becomes a portion of a greater landscape.

I cannot expect you to hear what I hear or see what I
see
or to share in the wonderment of it all.

But that's O.K.

I just wanted you to know there's a reason
why I'm here.

Igniting Originality Through Humor

Enhancing the creative factor of originality is easily accessible through humor.

Homographs

Homographs are words that are spelled the same but have different meanings and different origins.

Directions: Create in a single drawing a merger of meanings with a set of homographs.

Example: "A homograph horn"

horn: a wind instrument
horn: a structure protruding from the head of certain mammals.

Try some of these:

A homograph school	A homograph jerky
A homograph bark	A homograph nail
A homograph sock	A homograph punch
A homograph palm	A homograph saw
A homograph date	A homograph pop
A homograph lock	A homograph hamper

There are many, many homographs. Here are a few that can extend originality in both humor and thought.

arms:	a part of the body	jam:	fruit that has been preserved
arms:	weapons	jam:	to squeeze into something
bat:	a piece of baseball equipment; a club	list:	a grouping of words, symbols, etc.
bat:	a flying mammal	list:	to lean or tilt to one side
bill:	money owed	mole:	a condition found on the skin
bill:	part of bird; beak	mole:	a kind of animal
bowl:	play the game of bowling	pitcher:	a baseball position
bowl:	a dish	pitcher:	container for pouring liquid
Chow:	type of dog	pool:	a place to swim
chow:	slang for food	pool:	a game
dresser:	one who puts on clothes	root:	underground part of a plant
dresser:	a bureau	root:	to cheer for someone or something
elder:	someone older		
elder:	a kind of tree	stalk:	follow secretly
fan:	a device for cooling	stalk:	main stem of a plant
fan:	an admirer	yak:	a kind of animal
		yak:	talk endlessly

Writing Articles from Provided Topics

Newspaper-type headline topics can promote humor in imaginative and original ways. Use some of these suggestions for stimulating humor in your mind; then transfer the process to those realms affecting the lives of your students.

"Bus mechanic admits using peanut butter as a repair agent"
"Dr. Seuss becomes Superintendent of Schools"
"Student wins lifelong supply of school cafeteria lunches"
"Overdue schoolbook fine paid by 300-year-old man"
"Computer fails national achievement tests"
"Duplicated copies from school copy machine deemed toxic"
"School dictionaries banned by legislators"
"Recess extended five minutes with year-round school"
"Godzilla will speak to P.T.A."
"Noted psychiatrist says grades are dangerous to mental health"
"Principal's paddle installed in the Smithsonian Institute"
"Egyptian Hierglyphics and Greek to be taught to all preschoolers"

A sense of humor, at times, is as important as knowledge.

Developing newspaper-type headlines on familiar issues can be an exercise of satire. Utilize this opportunity to expand the concept and role of satire as applied to governmental and social issues. Investigate the role of literature, newspaper editorials and some television commentaries as agents of satire. Speculate on what elements of satire might be found in the books of Dr. Seuss. For example, what do you suppose the *Grinches* really represent? Commercialism of Christmas? Uniformity? Something else?

Embellished Alliteration

Alliteration is the usage of two or more words containing the same initial sound in a phrase, sentence or line of speech. Select certain concepts, academic or otherwise, and have students write a complete line utilizing the same beginning letter.

> Carl carelessly creates creative creatures creatively.
> Margaret moves many mentally made molecules magically.

Many statements of this type can lead to interesting interpretive analyses. As an example, is carelessness an element of risk-taking associated with highly creative people? Are molecules more of a human perception or a graphically objective perception of matter?

Humor is, for the most part, formulating associations in unique, novel and sometimes original ways. Many of the original "free-play" sketches done by Rembrandt would certainly indicate a sense of humor within his highly creative mind.

Riddles Through Shared Attributes

Begin by associating attributes of typical school-related items.

Examples: cafeteria table—accommodates food, four legs
cafeteria—where students eat, where food is served
chalkboard—written on with chalk, can be erased
fire drill—buzzer, exit doors
volleyball—rubber, bounces, spherical
class—where students learn, doors, wall, a group of kids
teacher—teaches, supervises, arms, legs, mind, etc.
students—study, learn, arms, legs, heads, minds, etc.
homework—additional schoolwork assigned for home

Many attributes will occur in one's mind when phrasing questions.

1. What has a buzzer and over several hundred legs?
   Answer: kids responding to a fire drill

2. What goes "shhhhhhhhh" down a hallway?
   Answer: a teacher supervising her class

3. What is carried under one's arm and causes forgetfulness?
   Answer: homework

4. _____

   _____

5. _____

   _____

6. _____

   _____

7. _____

   _____

Invention, Humor and Originality

Using invention and humor will generate extremely unique patterns of thought.

Try this with children or adults.

Directions: Piece together an invention that would function as one of the following:

a teacher   a parent
a pizza delivery service   a friend
a housecleaning service   a librarian
a principal   a school bus driver
a baby-sitting service   something else?

Each piece utilized must have a purpose. Either explain the purpose when asked or prepare a written description on how the robot contraption functions. Additional pieces may be drawn and added to the invention.

For a dramatic effect, have students paste together the parts on black construction paper. This is an axample from David, a talented fifth grade student. His written description is as follows:

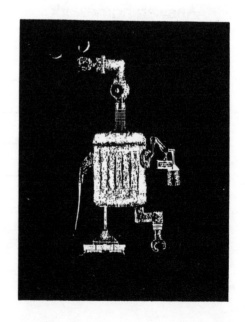

This unusual robot serves as a teacher. It's a state-of-the-art product that gives a stress-free and long-lasting performance. My teacher-robot uses an electrically charged prod to discipline students. The skateboard is used for traveling, the credit card for buying supplies the school did not budget and the trash can as a body and computer network. The suction plunger and vise grip squeeze attachment serves as an arm and the mechanical hand for collecting undesirable items students bring from home. The heat-seeking motion detector serves as eyes. The hydraulic neck is used to peer over shelves and other tall items and provides a cushion for traveling over the bumps in the school's tile.

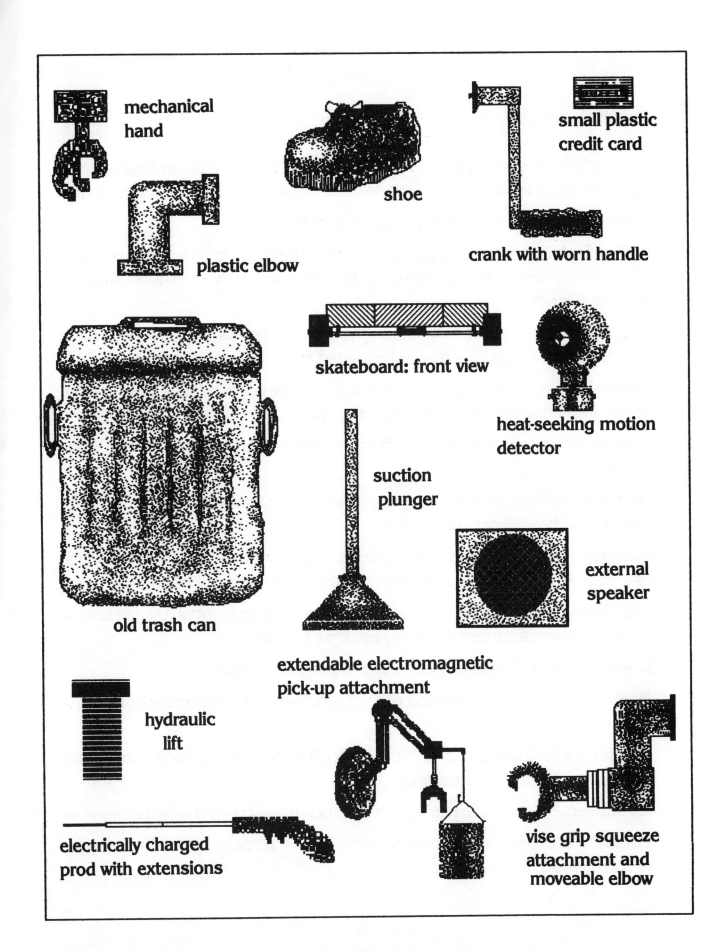

mechanical hand

shoe

small plastic credit card

plastic elbow

crank with worn handle

skateboard: front view

heat-seeking motion detector

suction plunger

old trash can

external speaker

extendable electromagnetic pick-up attachment

hydraulic lift

electrically charged prod with extensions

vise grip squeeze attachment and moveable elbow

Robotic Words

For students really involved in robotics, provide these terms and definitions. This should provide a really high tech description of their created robots.

Android: A kind of robot made to appear human

Artificial intelligence: The study of making computers do "intelligent things." There is dispute among authorities as to what consists of intelligent behavior and intelligence.

Feedback: Data received by a computer from the robot about the robot and its surroundings. The data is forwarded by sensors on the robot.

Gears: Stationed between the motor and that part of a robot it drives. They generally increase or decrease the motor speed.

Gripper or end effector: The mechanism attached to a robot's arm to hold things

Hydraulic system: Device using a special oil in cylinders and pipes to drive certain mechanical parts of a robot

Interface: A connection between a robot and its computer to convert electrical impulses from the computer into commands for the robot or vice versa

Lead-through programming: Method of instructing a robot by guiding it through movements necessary to perform a function

Logo: Computer language often used to program robots

Machine vision: A primitive kind of sight produced by a computer-controlled device

Navigation: Information used by a computer from the robot's sensors to guide the robot in its movements

Odometer: A sensor measuring the distance traveling by a wheeled vehicle

Photoelectric cell: An electronic device which detects light; often a part of a sensor on robots

Pitch: Name for the vertical movement in a robot's wrist, similar to the movement of a lever

Pneumatic system: A device powered by air or a certain gas to operate the gripper or another mechanical part of a robot

Port: A socket on a computer where interfaces and other kinds of electronic equipment are plugged in

Program: Instructional sequences that are given to a computer controlling a robot's functions

Robot: A computer-controlled machine programmed to do functions

Roll: A specific movement of a robot's wrist; a side-by-side movement

Sensor: A device that gives a robot's computer information about the robot and its immediate surroundings

Sonar sensor: Used for navigation usually, this sensor emits a sound and "listens" for a returning echo. The echo is a bounce-back from obstacles in the robot's surroundings. Distance is then measured by the time taken for the sound to return.

Speech synthesizer: An electronic device that can be programmed to produce words and sentences through a speaker system. The device is usually a chip.

Transformer: An electronic device which converts electricity to voltage suitable for powering things

Turtle: A micro-robot on wheels programmed to draw and move about through a computer language

Working envelope: Area of space a robot's arm is capable of reaching

Yaw: Name given to the movement of a robot's wrist from left to right or vice versa

Invention, Humor and Originality: A Few Extensions

Consider some of these follow-ups to the invention on the previous page.

1. If the trash can was used, draw the mechanisms that could only be seen from the inside. Do either a top view (if the lid was removed) or a side view perspective.

2. What kinds of categories of work would you anticipate humanoids or robots to perform in the year 2500?

3. Place two completed robots together and combine functions. What new kinds of functions could the combined robots serve?

4. Place two completed robots together on a bulletin board. Label one "a protagonist." Label the other one "an antagonist." Establish a setting, such as grocery supermarket or a hardware store. Create, in writing, a small scenario, that would reflect the meanings of the words *protagonist* and *antagonist.* In doing so develop the personalities of the two machines, for example, aggressiveness vs. cooperativeness, serious-minded vs. fun-loving, etc. Or, using the information above, role-play the situation with two volunteer students assuming the roles of the two robots.

Combining Personality Traits Through Invention

Take discarded magazines that are full of photographs. Have students select well-known faces such as politicians, actors, singers, etc. Take the photographs and cut them in strips and piece together the perfect *politician* or the perfect *actor* or the perfect *musician,* using construction paper and glue. Respond to this statement afterwards: Considering the faces you used, provide a rationale for the conglomerate you created. What makes it perfect as a politician or an actor or a musician?

Discuss: What makes a face important?

Invention S-t-r-e-t-c-h

Circle an item from this column to improve.

Circle one or two items from this column for the improvement.

radio	rubber
athletic shoes	springs
pogo stick	pockets
bicycle	plastic
skateboard	set of directions
pencil	wheels
stereo	hinges
balloon	fans
notebook	elastic
piggy bank	batteries
toothbrush	slogans
toy transformers	colors
textbook	motor
hat	lights
doll	hooks
Frisbee	gauges
beach ball	movement
hair dryer	texture
hula hoop	taste
television	Velcro
toy airplanes	suction

Circle one or two items from this listing to make it . . .

stretch	deflate	spin	bend	foamy
twist	jump	rotate	teach	pop up
compress	move	thin	thick	soft
bounce	dark	light	transparent	explode
fold	glow	sticky	adjustable	swivel
swivel	recline	magnetic	loud	flicker
whirl	chewable	talk	roll	float
rock	shake	squeeze	dissolve	soft
lighter	musical	learn	calculate	smile

Now improve the item with the attributes selected. Draw it and describe what it can do now.

93

Options:

1. Try creating homograph illustrations on words that really have multiple origins.

2. Peruse *Steven Caney's Invention Book* (1985) for some excellent ideas in nurturing original thinking, especially those sections on fantasy inventions. For inventing unique kinds of classroom things, see *Inventors Workshop* by Alan J. McCormack (1981) and *Inventioneering* by Bob Stanish and Carol Singletary (1987). For extending inventiveness into the realms of humor and broad areas of understanding, see *The Unconventional Invention Book* (Stanish, 1981).

3. Role-play the kinds of sounds certain punctuation symbols and other symbols would make if they could make sounds.

   What kind of a sound would an exclamation mark make?
   What kind of a sound would a comma make?
   What kind of a sound would a semicolon make?
   How about a dollar sign?
   How about a percentage symbol?
   How about parentheses?
   How about question marks and periods and quotation marks?
   How about colons and dashes?

   Read a selected nursery rhyme with punctuation sounds.

> Perhaps if you can find humor in yourself and not at the expense of others, others will find humor in themselves and not at the expense of others. And together, you, the world and I can smile at one moment in time. So many good things begin with a smile.

4. Add additional words to the three lists in "Invention S-t-r-e-t-c-h" for more item improvement and for additional flexibility.

5. Do Rube Goldberg kinds of inventions in drawings.

   Consider some of these topics with a minimum of at least five sequential events:

   - A gentle way to tickle an armadillo's stomach

   - A way to turn down a neighbor's loud blaring stereo that's positioned in a driveway

   - A way to get a stuck frog out of a house gutter pipe

   - A way to scare away a car thief who is tinkering with the family car

   - A convenient way of letting a family member know he or she is talking too long on the phone

   - A way to retrieve the morning paper that's thrown in the wrong yard

   - A way to make vacant a bathroom

   - A way to let a driver know he or she is too close to your car's bumper

   - A convenient way to stop loud snoring

   - A way to exercise your dog

   - A convenient way to time your suntan

   - A way to dry off a visitor on a rainy day before he or she enters the house

   - A way to turn on the lawn sprinkler while you're at the kitchen table

   - An unnoticeable way of picking up strands of spaghetti off your lap

   - A reminder system for forgetful shoppers

The Heritage Bestowed

Be it branching foliage within forests or the meanders of rivers and streams or the territorial claims of a species or the human capacity to accumulate and extend, we share a common heritage.

The heritage was bestowed with the unification of atoms to form molecules and from cells combining to form colonies. It was nurtured by plant forms and natural forces and by animal forms forming colonies and groupings of their kind. It was nurtured by men and women forming families and from families into clans from clans into communities and from communities into nations. In each, the extension into space was accomplished—usually in a competitive struggle but sometimes without struggle.

I can understand the child who extends his identity among his kind as I can understand the politicians who extend their power among their kind. Knowing this has helped me to understand myself and to find words to extend my creative essence and thought. It is with the metaphor that I understand and it is without struggle that I extend. Should my extensions be perceived as an intrusion into the space of others, it was never intended to be that. It is just the branching extensions of my inner structure. This requires not physical space for me, just space to be and space to become.

Guiding Fantasy Towards Expressive Poetic Language

Directions: Find a comfortable place to sit with paper and pen or pencil. Close your eyes and take a deep breath and slowly exhale. Allow your body to relax and breathe in once more and slowly breathe out. Allow your mind to take a scenic excursion along wooded pathways or of a coastline or of a white water stream.

Take a few seconds and allow your mind to image the sights and sounds of this excursion.

Open your eyes and now list on paper some specific things you saw.

Things I saw in my mind's eyes:

_____

_____

_____

_____

_____

_____

_____

Select any numeral between **1 and 10** and select any letter between **A and J**. Write the numeral and letter on paper. Write the phrase from the column on the next page that corresponds with your selected numeral.

1. The awareness
2. The thought
3. The loneliness
4. The image
5. The reality
6. The recollection
7. The illusion
8. The vision
9. The presence
10. The essence

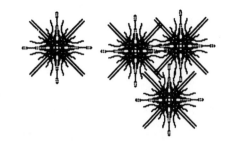

Example: (7) The illusion

Now select one item you listed on the excursion that you saw in your mind's eye and place the preposition *of* in front of this item. Write the item with the preposition *of* after the beginning phrase.

Example: The illusion *of sand castles*

Next find the phrase associated with the letter you selected. Write the phrase after the last phrase written.

A. is like the inner me.
B. was like a promised recalled
C. was like a melody played
D. is like a keepsake.
E. is like something valued.
F. was like a precious dream.
G. is like a friend.
H. is like a whisper.
 I. was like a traveler's return.
J. was like a memory recalled.

If J was selected, then the statement would be:

Example: The illusion of sand castles *was like a memory recalled.*

Now write the complete sentence.

_____

Think of a scene that could have caused the thought, and softly in your mind's eye caress the image. Take a deep breath and then exhale. Allow sensory words to formulate, words that apply to the senses. Try to begin this sentence with an *ing* word.

Example: The illusion of sand castles was like a memory recalled. *Feeling* the warmth of sun and sand, the illusion disappeared but came again with the ocean's spew.

Now write the two sentences as a paragraph.

_____

_____

_____

Allow the paragraph to settle in your mind's eye.

Extend the concepts by integrating relaxation with the imagery of the scene. Extend the paragraph into another paragraph and into another. See what you have created and share this creation with others.

Background

Several strategies are involved in this activity. **Guided fantasy** or **guided** or **directed imagery** is one. These are imaginary responses stimulated by a verbal scene provoked by a facilitator, group leader or teacher. Guided fantasy types of activities can be found in several publications such as *Experiences in Visual Thinking* (McKim, 1972) and *Scamper* (Eberle, 1971).

The respondent in this activity, after the introduction by the leader or teacher, uses **self-directed fantasy**, a variation of guided fantasy. Self-directed fantasy is where much of the imagery factors is supplied by the respondents. **Mental imagery** (McKim, 1971), the second category of McKim's types of imagery for visual thinking, is provided here. This imagery is constructed in the mind and the data utilized, in this instance, for written expression. According to McKim, three kinds of imagery are necessary for visual thinking. The first is **perceptual imagery** or what one sensory experiences in the world. A third type is that of **graphic imagery.** Graphic imagery deals with drawn images and symbols as a means of assisting conceptual understandings and communication. This processing is enhanced by opening access to the right side of the human brain. See *Drawing on the Right Side of the Brain* (Edwards, 1979).

Also embedded in the activity is that of **force-fit** or **forced relationship** or **forced association**. Force-fit is the heartline of the creative process. By forcing a relationship between elements, new combinations and thoughts occur. The force-fit aspect of this activity entertains a certain degree of randomness, which is referred to elsewhere in this book as random-fit.

Additional applications of force-fit can be found in this book in "Invention, Humor and Originality" and "Invention S-t-r-e-t-c-h."

Options:

1. In writing descriptive narratives, establish tone and setting through techniques of guided fantasy and self-directed fantasy. Do not overuse the technique, but for initiating a beginning effort, it may prove extremely valuable.

2. Use the techniques of this activity for combining completed sentences into a poetic structure. Provide this as a challenge to a group of students.

3. Using magazine photographs create a collage that would express the visual impact of the student paragraphs.

4. Extend with additional words both columns of the 1-10 list and the A-J list for additional options.

5. Have students interpret their paragraphs as to meaning through the personal experiences of their own lives.

6. Try music along with guided fantasies, but be selective as to what is played. Slow, melodic instrumentals of a classical nature appear most appropriate—especially music of the Far East.

7. Try guided fantasy techniques with cinquain, haiku, tanka and other poetic structures.

8. Share some of the statements associated with the photographs in this book among students. In what ways might completed sentences and paragraphs be used with the development of posters addressing topics of concern?

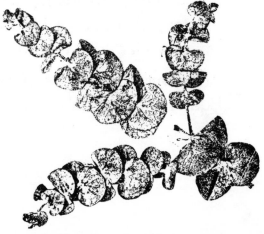

9. The mood of this activity may accommodate an introspective view of self. Consider using some of these multiple choice questions.

Consider the following:
a plant vine
a sunrise
a sunset
an incoming tide
an outgoing tide
a seashell
a sun cloud
a rain cloud
a mountainside
a bud
a seed
a flower
a piece of driftwood

Select one of the above for each blank line and provide an explanation for each.

My outer self is most like _____ because

My inner self is most like _____ because

I would prefer to be most like _____ because

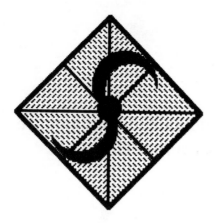

Symbolizing Self

This exercise deals with a figural representation of self. It is suggested that several additional copies of the grid "Symbol of Self" be made available to participants.

Guidelines and Directions:

Review Options page prior to doing this activity.

General: Participants are to familiarize themselves with the patterns provided on the Legend page and the meanings associated with colors. Using patterns and colors, a symbol of self is created on the grid.

Specific:

- Determine what patterns would best represent the present self. Combinations of patterns may be used.

- Determine what colors and their meanings would best represent self with the created patterns.

- Complete the symbol with patterns and colors on the provided grid.

Legend

Diamond:

Reflects and shines; adaptable; can be redesigned.

Square:

Firm and secure; boundaries are set.

Polygon:

Versatile; many-sided with capacity to produce more angles. Functions within the boundaries it creates.

Explosion:

Unique and varied; trajectories extend out from the center. Sometimes set by boundaries, sometimes not.

Spiral:

Unpredictable; movements can run contrary. High energy level.

Color Code:
- Blues and purples reflect vision.
- Yellows and oranges reflect creativeness.
- Greens and browns reflect growth.
- Reds reflect objectivity and detail.

Symbol of Self

Options:

- Draw a single pattern on the grid.
- Draw several patterns on the grid.
- Draw combined patterns on the grid.
- Draw portions of combined patterns on the grid.
- Draw patterns within patterns on the grid.

The total image should be reflective of you in pattern and color.

Refer to the legend for meanings associated with patterns and colors.

Options:

1. Consider using this activity for in-service training programs.

2. In a group or class, have participants create their symbols without name identification. Then have participants attempt to identify symbols with those who created them.

3. After creating symbols, have participants match created symbols similar to their own, then discuss similarities of focus.

4. Consider doing two symbols, one that represents *an ideal* and one representing *the here and now.*

5. Consider this activity as a pre-counseling exercise prior to individual student counseling.

Within most of us is an essence of radiating warmth and goodness. When information is processed from our mind centers and transmitted to our heart centers, it is of great value. This nucleus of mind and heart may be the deep reality of basic truth. It is better to act upon information that has been processed by mind and heart.

Brainstorming: Some Varied Ways

There are so many varied ways of generating ideas. This section summarizes some popular ways found in business and industry. It is not unusual to look at this realm since group brainstorming, as we know it today, was designed by a man of advertising. A few of the ways mentioned are not, in a sense, brainstorming techniques. But they do accommodate and integrate with many of the other techniques listed here. The list below is not complete, but it does contain techniques that are extremely useable in a classroom. Two exceptional sources of information were used in compiling this list: Arthur B. VanGundy's very comprehensive book *Techniques of Structured Problem Solving* (VanGundy, 1981) and *Idea Power: Time Tested Methods to Stimulate Your Imagination* by Morris O. Edwards (Edwards, 1986).

• Battelle Bildmappen Brainwriting

Developed by the Battelle Institute of Frankfurt, West Germany, this technique accommodates a small group of five to eight participants. After brainstorming several solutions to a provided problem, a folder of ten pictures is given to the group. The pictures are unrelated to the problem and simply may be taken from magazines. Each group member writes ideas on paper stimulated by the pictures. The ideas stimulated then are presented to the group for clarification and refinement.

• Brainstorming

See page 49 in this book for more comprehensive information. Group brainstorming is an easy way of generating ideas. It is based on the concept of deferred judgment, that is, generate many ideas first, then sort out, refine and decide later. Brainstorming has many variations to accommodate a variety of interests and problems. Group brainstorming is often referred to as *brainstorming.*

• Brainwriting

Refer to page 4. This is the silent production of ideas on paper by group members. This process is particularly effective in large groups when there may be participants who have the potential for dominating the group. It is often combined with classical brainstorming or other structured forms of brainstorming.

• Brainwriting Pool

This is a brainwriting variation from the Battelle Institute of West Germany. Within a small group, members silently write ideas to a problem on sheets of paper. Upon the completion of four ideas by each member, the papers are placed on a table or desk. Each member then takes a different paper from the table and adds additional ideas. After a few minutes, the papers are returned to the table. The process repeats itself until there is a quantity of ideas.

> We must assume the responsibility, as teachers, to teach children how to think. It is a tragedy that most schools are so involved in their instructional planning that the ingredient that accommodates all skill development is not planned, and that is, the skill of thinking.

• Checklists

A checklist is a device, consisting of words, whose primary purpose is to stimulate additional ideas to a problem or situation. Checklists are extremely valuable as compliments to brainstorming techniques. Alex Osborn's **seventy-three idea-spurring questions** was the first major checklist to have impact as an ideational device. Others of special note would be Gary Davis' checklist drawn, in part, from Osborn's list and Bob Eberle's *scamper*, a summary of Osborn's list. See page 46 in this book for the reproduction of *scamper*.

• Crawford Slip Writing Technique

This technique works effectively in larger groups, like thirty or so members. Group members are given small slips of paper. A problem statement is read by the leader, teacher or facilitator. Ideas to the solution of the problem are written on the small slips of paper—one idea per slip. After approximately ten minutes, the slips are collected, sorted and placed in categories of frequency or similarity and usability. Ideas that are deemed the most appropriate to the problem are then selected.

• Focused Object

This technique was designed by Charles S. Whiting and uses ideas stimulated by forcing a fit or forcing an association between a constant element and random elements. Variations of this approach can be found throughout the activities of this book. A constant element relating to a problem is presented and then a random element is selected. Using the two elements in combination, associations are then made for the purpose of stimulating idea solutions. After ideation appears to be complete on one random element, then another random element is combined with the constant element for additional ideas.

Problem-solving approaches
can be applied in any classroom.
They can apply across any discipline of learning.
To address a problem of the past with alternative solutions
is just as important to the
development of thinking as addressing problems today
with alternative solutions.

• Gallery Method

Ideas are individually and silently written on paper, then taped to a wall. Group members, after a break, peruse the posted ideas much like art patrons view works in an art gallery. In returning to their groups, individuals again silently write ideas on paper. The effect is that posted ideas viewed are likely to stimulate additional ideas. The process continues until a significant number of ideas are posted on the wall.

• Green Light-Red Light Brainstorming

Also known as *alternating brainstorming,* this technique requires ideating for a few minutes and then rating the ideas. Follow the rating period with more brainstorming. Continue the process until there is an adequate quantity of ideas.

• Method 635

Method 635 is one of the earliest brainwriting methods. The numbers relate to six people producing three ideas each in five minutes. There are many variations of this technique. The basic premise requires writing ideas on paper, then after five minutes, giving them to a person sitting alongside. The ideas received are either developed further or new ideas added. The process continues for five rounds or until each participant receives his original paper.

> Methods of brainstorming should
> vary because of the differences in
> hemispheric modes of
> perceiving and being.

• Mind Mapping

A variation of brainwriting, this technique involves writing the problem on the center portion of paper, and then using webbing strategies to branch out from the problem with lines, arrows, and words within spheres. Viewing ideas both in a semantic and figural sense can extend and stimulate associations. The use of light-colored markers on the webbing structure can also promote classification or categorization of concepts.

• Nominal Group Technique

A problem or problem statement is presented orally to a group. Group members silently list ideas on paper for a period of approximately five minutes. The ideas are then listed on the chalkboard in a rotational basis—one idea from each participant. Discussion follows for clarification. Ideas are then ranked according to priority or importance by each group member on paper. A total tally is then taken for the best ideas.

• Phillips 66

Within a large group, smaller groups of approximately six members are created. Each small group brainstorms the provided topic for six minutes. A member from each group presents the major ideas of that group. These ideas are discussed and clarified with the total group. These ideas are also accepted at this time. New groups are formed consisting of a different composition of members for additional work on the ideas, again for a six-minute time limit.

• Pin Cards

This is a variation of brainwriting in which groups of five to eight members list ideas on small index cards. One idea per member is written on a single card. Each completed card is passed to the person sitting on the right. A new idea may be written on the card received. If the received idea stimulates a different idea, then a card is taken from the person sitting on the left. The stimulated idea is then written on the received card and either retained or passed to the person sitting on the right. After thirty minutes the cards are collected and pinned to a bulletin board or taped to a wall. Ideas are then sorted into categories and column headings made. Group members read all cards and move appropriate ones to different categories to adjust for duplications. Group clarification or ideas are then provided.

• SIL Method

Developed at the Battelle Institute, SIL is an acronym for **Successive Integration of Problem Elements,** as translated from German. A brainstorming and brainwriting variation, it combines the elements of free association and forced association or force-fit. In small groups, individuals generate ideas on paper. After two ideas are read by two group members, the small group attempts to integrate the two ideas into one idea. After the third idea is read by the third group member, an attempt is made to integrate all three ideas into a single idea or possible solution. The process continues until all ideas are tried for an integrated solution. The method is culminated when an acceptable integrated solution is found.

> **Regardless of the technique, problem statements should be structured to begin with . . . In what ways might we or I . . . or How might we or I . . . ?**

• Solo Brainstorming

This is individual brainstorming. At times this is expedient and useful, but the obvious drawbacks are the positive *freewheeling* and *piggybacking* aspects of group brainstorming.

• Stimulus Analysis

This technique, also from the Battelle Institute, is appropriate for solo brainstorming and small group brainstorming. A list of ten concrete words are selected unrelated to the problem. Each word is described in terms of its attributes and an attempt is made to force-fit each of the word descriptors or attributes into a problem solution. After a word has been used completely, the next word is used.

**So many ideas that have stayed for centuries
were highly criticized in their times.**

• Stop and Go Brainstorming

This technique is that of brainstorming in spurts. By providing periodic rest stops, new ideas are stimulated in the mind.

• Trigger Method

This is a combined brainstorming and brainwriting technique where, in small groups, individual ideas are written on paper for a five-minute period of time. Group members then read their ideas to the group. A discussion period is then held with the anticipation that new ideas or variations on the ideas presented will be triggered. The process continues until all ideas are presented orally.

• Visual Brainstorming

As implied, this technique deals with sketching out ideas to a problem. Some very interesting photographs of this technique can be seen in Robert McKim's book *Thinking Visually* (1980).

● Visual Synectics

Developed at the Battelle Institute, visual synectics uses pictures whose topics are unrelated to the problem. In small groups, members describe what they see in pictures. After responses have been recorded, the group attempts to relate these response elements to the problem's solution. It is best when using pictures in this technique, to select pictures that depict motion.

Man's greatest achievement was, is, and will be —the idea.

Options:

1. Try these approaches whenever possible. Note how some students seem to respond more effectively to brainwriting than with brainstorming. Note how some students seem to respond ideationally more to a visual stimulus than a verbal one. By using a variety of idea-generating methods, there should be a greater accommodation of student hemispheric differences.

2. Try combining several approaches for a new entity. Literally, hundreds of variations may be created from the techniques provided.

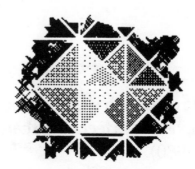

A Pre-epilogue of Sorts

In the early castles were the great halls. These were areas of great proportions where entertainment and feasts and celebrations took place. The great halls were warmed by a fire on the central hearth. In time, the hearths were moved closer to a wall and then into a wall where passages were made. The passages were called fireplaces.

At a much later time, when small dwellings were made of log and stone, good hearthstone made better fireplaces. It was not unusual to take the remnants of an old dwelling for use in a new. Good hearthstone traveled and well it should. For near the hearthstone and to the accompaniment of fire shadows, ideas and dreams appeared.

And it is, within my mind, that hearthstone is appropriate for a title. My hearthstone has and will always be the creative processes. For it travels well and makes for good teaching and stretches the mind for more ideas and dreams.

Take from within this book, what travels well with you.

Bob Stanish

Confine
plant forms to
a container and you will
know exactly the dimensions
they shall reach.

Confine

your teachers to your
restricting curricula
and your paperwork
and you will know exactly the dimensions
they shall reach.

And

each budding branch and each extending child shall not
extend far beyond the perimeters of
their confinement.

Space

determines the shape
of all living things.

References
and Suggested Readings

Biondi, Angelo M., and Parnes, Sidney J., eds. *Assessing Creative Growth.* Buffalo, New York: Bearly Limited, 1976.

Biondi, Angelo M. *Have an Affair with Your Mind.* Great Neck, New York: Creative Synergetic Associates, Ltd., 1974.

Biondi, Angelo M., ed. *The Creative Process.* Buffalo, New York: D.O.K. Publishers, Inc., 1972.

Buzan, Tony. *Use Both Sides of Your Brain.* New York: E.P. Dutton, 1983.

Caney, Steven. *Steven Caney's Invention Book.* New York: Workman Publishing, 1985.

Crawford, Robert P. *The Techniques of Creative Thinking.* Englewood Cliffs, New Jersey: Prentice-Hall, 1954.

de Bono, Edward. *Lateral Thinking: Creativity Step by Step.* New York: Harper & Row, 1973.

de Mille, Richard. *Put Your Mother on the Ceiling: Children's Imagination Games.* New York: Walker & Company, 1967.

Davis, Gary A. *Creativity Is Forever,* 2nd edition. Dubuque, Iowa: Kendall/ Hunt Publishing Company, 1986.

_____ . *Idea Checklist for Stimulating Solutions,* Chapter 3: "Have an Affair with Your Mind," Angelo M. Biondi, ed. Buffalo, New York: Bearly Limited, 1974.

Eberle, Bob. *Help in Solving Problems Creatively at Home and School.* Carthage, Illinois: Good Apple, Inc., 1984.

_____ . *Scamper: Games for Imagination Development.* Buffalo, New York: D.O.K. Publishers, Inc., 1971.

_____ . *Scamper-On for Creative Imagination Development.* Buffalo, New York: D.O.K. Publishers, Inc., 1984.

_____ . *Visual Thinking: A "Scamper" Tool for Useful Imaging.* Buffalo, New York: D.O.K. Publishers, Inc., 1982.

Eberle, Bob, and Stanish, Bob. *CPS for Kids: A Resource Book for Teaching Creative Problem Solving to Children.* Buffalo, New York: D.O.K. Publishers, Inc., 1980.

Edwards, Betty. *Drawing on the Right Side of the Brain.* Los Angeles: J.P. Tarcher, Inc., 1979.

Edwards, Morris O. *Idea Power: Time Tested Methods to Stimulate Your Imagination.* Buffalo, New York: Bearly Limited, 1986.

Feldhusen, John F., and Treffinger, Donald J. *Creative Thinking and Problem Solving in Gifted Education*, 3rd edition. Dubuque, Iowa: Kendall/Hunt Publishing Company, 1985.

Franck, Frederick. *The Zen of Seeing.* New York: Vintage Books, a division of Random House, 1973.

Gordon, W.J.J., and Poze, Tony. *Strange and Familiar.* Cambridge, Massachusetts: SES Associates, 1972.

Gordon, W.J.J. *Synectics.* New York: Harper & Row, 1961.

Gowan, John C., Khatena, Joe, and Torrance, E. Paul, eds. *Creativity: Its Educational Implications.* Dubuque, Iowa: Kendall/Hunt Publishing Company, 1985.

Gowan, John C. *Trance, Art and Creativity.* Northridge, California: Published by the author, 1975.

Guilford, J.P. *The Nature of Human Intelligence.* New York: McGraw-Hill, 1967.

_____ . *Way Beyond the I.Q.* Buffalo, New York: The Creative Education Foundation, 1977.

Isaksen, Scott G., and Treffinger, Donald J. *Creative Problem Solving: The Basic Course.* Buffalo, New York: Bearly Limited, 1985.

Khatena, Joe. *Imagery and Creative Imagination.* Buffalo, New York: Bearly Limited, 1984.

Levy, Nathan, Levy, Janet, and Edwards, Joan. *There Are Those.* Hightstown, New Jersey: N.L. Associates, Inc., 1982.

McCormack, Alan J. *Inventors Workshop.* Belmont, California: Fearon Teacher Aids, a division of David S. Lake Publishers, 1981.

MacKinnon, Donald W. *In Search of Human Effectiveness.* Buffalo, New York: Creative Education Foundation in association with Creative Synergetic Associates, Ltd., 1978.

McKim, Robert H. *Experiences in Visual Thinking.* Belmont, California: Wadsworth, 1972.

_____ . *Thinking Visually: A Strategy Manual for Problem Solving.* Belmont, California: Wadsworth, 1980.

Maslow, Abraham H. *Toward a Psychology of Being*, 2nd edition. Princeton, New Jersey: Van Nostrand, 1968.

Noller, Ruth B. *Scratching the Surface of Creative Problem Solving, a Bird's Eye View of CPS.* Buffalo, New York: D.O.K. Publishers, Inc., 1977.

Osborn, Alex F. *Applied Imagination.* New York: Charles Scribner's Sons, 1963.

Parnes, Sidney J. *A Facilitating Style of Leadership.* Buffalo, New York: Bearly Limited in association with The Creative Education Foundation, 1985.

_____ . *Magic of Your Mind.* Buffalo, New York: Bearly Limited, 1981.

Parnes, Sidney J., Noller, Ruth B., and Biondi, Angelo M. *Guide to Creative Action.* New York: Charles Scribner's Sons, 1977.

Potter, Tony, and Guild, Ivor. *Robotics.* London: Usborne Publishing, Ltd., 1983.

Prince, George M. "The Mindspring Theory," *The Journal of Creative Behavior,* 1975, 9(3), 159-181.

Renzulli, Joseph S. *The Enrichment Triad Model: A Guide for Developing Defensible Programs for the Gifted and Talented.* Wethersfield, Connecticut: Creative Learning Press, 1977.

Sanders, Donald A., and Sanders, Judith A. *Teaching Creativity Through Metaphor: An Integrated Brain Approach.* New York: Longman, Inc., 1984.

Shallcross, Doris J. *Teaching Creative Behavior.* Englewood Cliffs, New Jersey: Prentice-Hall, Inc., 1981.

Skaught, Benjamin J. "Songwriting Should Be Taught in Your Gifted Program," *The Gifted Child Today,* 1987, 10(1), 40-41.

Stanish, Bob. *I Believe in Unicorns: Classroom Experiences for Activating Creative Thinking.* Carthage, Illinois: Good Apple, Inc., 1979.

_____ . *Mindglow: Classroom Encounters with Creative Thinking.* Carthage, Illinois: Good Apple, Inc., 1986.

_____ . *Sunflowering: Thinking, Feeling, Doing Activities for Creative Thinking.* Carthage, Illinois: Good Apple, Inc., 1977.

_____ . *The Unconventional Invention Book: Classroom Activities for Activating Student Inventiveness.* Carthage, Illinois: Good Apple, Inc., 1981.

_____ . "The Underlying Structures and Thoughts About Randomness and Creativity." *The Journal of Creative Behavior,* 1986 20(2), 110-116.

Stanish, Bob, and Eberle, Bob. *Be a Problem Solver: A CPS Chartbook.* Buffalo, New York: D.O.K. Publishers, Inc., 1984.

Stanish, Bob, and Singletary, Carol. *Inventioneering: Nurturing Talent in the Classroom.* Carthage, Illinois: Good Apple, Inc., 1987.

Stevens, Peter S. *Patterns in Nature.* Boston: Little, Brown and Company in association with The Atlantic Monthly Press, 1974.

Sturner, William F. *Risking Change: Endings and Beginnings.* Buffalo, New York: Bearly, Limited, 1987.

Synectics, Inc. *Making It Strange*, Books 1-4. New York: Harper & Row, 1968.

Torrance, E. Paul. *Guiding Creative Talent.* Englewood Cliffs, New Jersey: Prentice-Hall, Inc., 1962.

_____ . *The Search for Satori and Creativity.* Buffalo, New York: The Creative Education Foundation, 1979.

Valentino, Catherine. *The Invention Convention.* Morristown, New Jersey: Silver Burdette Company, 1984.

VanGundy, Arthur B., Jr. *Managing Group Creativity: A Modular Approach to Problem Solving.* New York: American Management Associations, 1984.

VanGundy, Arthur B., Jr. *Techniques of Structured Problem Solving.* New York: Van Nostrand Reinhold Company, 1981.

Wayman, Joe, and Plum, Lorraine. *Secrets & Surprises.* Carthage, Illinois: Good Apple, Inc., 1977.

Whiting, Charles S. *Creative Thinking.* New York: Reinhold Publishing Co., 1958.

Williams, Frank E. *Classroom Ideas for Encouraging Thinking and Feeling.* Buffalo, New York: D.O.K. Publishers, Inc., 1970.

_____ . *The Second Volume of Classroom Ideas for Encouraging Thinking and Feeling.* Buffalo, New York: D.O.K. Publishers, Inc., 1982.

Index

Acceptance finding, 63
Alliteration, 86
Alternating brainstorming, see green light-red light brainstorming, 111
Analogy, 30-37, 77-78, 103
Analogy card game, 77-78
Analogy statements, 10
Applied Imagination, 49
Attribute listing, 7

Battelle Bildmappen brainwriting, 108
Battelle Institute, 4, 108-109, 112
Be a Problem Solver, 63
Brainstorming, 3, 49 (rules), 108-114
Brainstorming techniques, 4, 108-114
Brainwriting, 3-4, 108-109, 111-114
Brainwriting pool, 109
Branching (pattern), 20-27

Caney, Steven, 94
Checklists, see idea checklist
Cinquain, 2-4, (defined) 2, 10, 102
Classical brainstorming, 49, 109
Convergent production (defined), 67
Convergent thinking, 67
CPS, see Creative Problem-Solving
CPS for Kids, 63
CPSI, see Creative Problem-Solving Institute
Crawford, Robert, 7, 110
Crawford slip writing technique, 110
Creative Education Foundation (The), 63
Creative problem solving, 10, 63-64
Creative Problem-Solving: The Basic Course, 63
Creative Problem-Solving Institute (CPSI), 63
Creative thinking skills, 66
Creative thinking, 67
Creativity Is Forever, 42
Criterion items for an idea evaluation grid, 60-61

Data finding, 63
Davis, Gary, 42, 45, 109
Deferred judgment, 49
de Mille, Richard, 47, 67
Diamante (defined), 79-80
Diamond (pattern), 105
Direct analogy, 32-33
Directed imagery, see guided fantasy
Discovery by doing, 52-55
Discovery journals, 55
Divergent production (defined), 67
Divergent thinking, 67
Drawing on the Right Side of the Brain, 101
Duel ideating, 79-80
Eberle, Bob, 45, 47, 63, 67, 101, 109
Edwards, Morris, 108
Edwards, Betty, 101
Elaboration (thinking), 66
Excursions, see guided fantasy
Experiences in Visual Thinking, 101
Explosions (pattern), 20-27, 105
Expressive language, 98-100

Factors of creative thinking, 66
Fantasy analogy, 32
Flexible thinking, 66-67
Fluent thinking, 66-67
Focused object technique, 110
Force-fit, see forced association
Forced association, 101
Forced relationships, see forced association
Franck, Frederick, 10
Freewheeling, 113
Fuller, Buckminister, 65

Gallery method technique, 110
Generalizations (patterns), 26-27
Goldberg, Rube, 95
Gordon, William J.J., 31, 42
Graphic imagery, 101

Green light-red light brainstorming, 111
Group brainstorming, see brainstorming, brainstorming techniques, and classical brainstorming
Guided fantasy, 76, 98-103
Guided imagery, see guided fantasy
Guilford, J.P., 7, 67

Haiku, 10, (defined) 70, 70-72, 102
Homographs, 84-95, (defined) 84
Humor, 84-95, see also invention and humor

Idea checklist, 44-46, 49, 109
Idea evaluation grid, 60-62
Idea Power, 108
Idea-spurring questions, 45, 109
Ideational fluency techniques, 56-61
Ideational fluency, 67
Imagery, 10
Imaging, 8-11
Imagery and Creative Imagination, 10
Invention and forced association, 93
Invention and humor, 88-95
Inventioneering, 94
Inventors Workshop, 94
Isaksen, Scott, 63

Khatena, Joe, 10, 67
Levy, Nathan and Janet, 55
Lowell, James R., 16

Making It Strange, 32
McCormack, Alan, 94
McKim, Robert, 10, 67, 101, 113
Meanders (pattern), 20-27
Mental imagery, 101
Mess finding, 63
Metaphorical thinking, 38-43, (defined) 42,
Metaphorical thinking and problem solving, 40
Method 635 technique, 111
Modification techniques, see idea checklist
Mind mapping technique, 111
Mindglow, 56
Nominal group technique, 111
Objectives (patterns), 26-27
Originality (thinking), 66
Originality and humor, 84-95
Osborn, Alex, 45, 49, 63, 109
Osborn-Parnes method, 63 see also CPS

Parnes, Sidney, 63
Perceptual imagery, 101
Personal analogy, 32
Phillips 66 technique, 112
Piggybacking (defined) 57, 113
Pin card technique, 112
Polygon (pattern), 105

Poze, Tony, 42
Prince, George, 42
Problem finding, 63
Problem solving, 52-55, 64

Random events, 70-72
Random-fit, (defined) 71, 71-76, 101
Randomness, 70-72
Riddles (through shared attributes), 87
Robotic words, 90-91

Scamper, 45-49, 101, 109
Scamper checklist, 46
Self-directed fantasy, 101-102
SIL method technique, 112
Singletary, Carol, 94
Skaught, Benjamin J., 47
S.O.I., see structure of the intellect model
Solo brainstorming, 113
Solution finding, 63
"Songwriting Should Be Taught in Your Gifted Program," 47
Spirals (patterns), 26-27, 105
Square (pattern), 105
Stanish, Bob, 56, 63, 66, 94
Starfish design, 56-61, 64
Steven Caney's Invention Book, 94
Stimulus analysis technique, 113
Stop and go brainstorming, 113
Story writing and symbolic analogy, 34
Structure (defined), 26, 70-72
Structure of the intellect model, 67
Symbol of self, 104-107
Symbolic analogy, 32, 34-37
Synectics, 10, (defined) 31

Tanka, 10, (defined) 72, 102
Techniques of Structured Problem Solving, 108
There Are Those, 55
Thinking Visually, 10, 113
Torrance, E. Paul, 49, 66
Transformations, 67
Treffinger, Donald, 63
Trigger method technique, 113
Tzu, Lao, 17
Unconventional Invention Book (The), 94

VanGundy, Arthur B., 4-5, 108
Visual brainstorming, 113
Visual imagery, 10
Visual synectics technique, 114
Visual thinking, 101
Visualization, 67
"Why" questions, 16
Whiting, Charles S., 110
Williams, Frank, 66
Zen of Seeing (The), 10

How do you measure silver threads of gossamer
that sway in an autumn's wind?

How do you measure the glisten of ice crystals
frozen to a window's pane?

How do you measure a flickering shadow
born by a candle's flame?

Measure them by the hearthstone
where fire shadows set ideas and dreams to play.

The Hearthstone Traveler